# NEW BELIEVER'S GUIDE TO
## *Effective Christian Living*

# New Believer's
## GUIDE TO
## EFFECTIVE CHRISTIAN LIVING

# GREG LAURIE

TYNDALE
MOMENTUM®

*A Tyndale nonfiction imprint*

Visit Tyndale online at newlivingtranslation.com
and tyndale.com.

*TYNDALE,* Tyndale's quill logo, *Tyndale Momentum,* and the
Tyndale Momentum logo are registered trademarks of Tyndale
House Ministries. Tyndale Momentum is the nonfiction imprint
of Tyndale House Publishers, Carol Stream, Illinois.

*New Believer's Guide to Effective Christian Living*

Cover design by David Riley Associates, Corona Del Mar,
California.

For information about special discounts for bulk purchases,
please contact Tyndale House Publishers at csresponse@
tyndale.com, or call 1-800-323-9400.

**Library of Congress Cataloging-in-Publication Data**

Laurie, Greg.
  New believer's guide to effective Christian living / by
Greg Laurie.
    p. cm.
  ISBN 978-0-8423-5574-2
  1. Christian life   I. Title
  BV4501.3 .L38 2002
  248.4—dc21                                    2002000557

Printed in Canada

28   27   26   25   24   23
22   21   20   19   18   17

# Table of Contents

# Part One

## JESUS IS MY SAVIOR

*Now he has made all of this plain to us by the coming of Christ Jesus, our Savior, who broke the power of death and showed us the way to everlasting life through the Good News.*

—2 TIMOTHY 1:10

## How "Being Saved" Makes
## Me Different

Welcome to the family! You are a new believer, and you have joined the family of God! We're glad you're here. Now maybe you're wondering what exactly has happened to you. Well, I'm glad you asked!

You have been "saved"! That means you were headed toward death, but now you're safe and sound.

We can probably all remember someone coming up to us sometime in our life with a wild look in his eyes and exclaiming, "Are you saved?"

We may have laughed it off, thinking it was such a sensationalistic term to use. After all, before coming to Jesus you weren't in a burning house or lost at sea. You were just living life one day at a time. Sure, it wasn't as good as you wanted it to be, but you weren't in a desperate situation.

Or at least you didn't think you were.

But in reality, the term "saved" is a very apt description of what happens to people who put their faith in Jesus Christ. Your real situation was actually worse than being in a burning house or a stormy sea. Before coming to Christ, you were separated from God and on your way to a certain judgment in a very real place called hell! But God reached out to you and, quite literally, saved you. The Bible uses that word to describe what happened:

- Jesus came to "*save* his people from their sins" (Matthew 1:21).
- "I am not ashamed of the gospel, because it is the power of God for the *salvation* of everyone who believes" (Romans 1:16, NIV).
- "There is *salvation* in no one else! There is no other name in all of heaven for people to call on to *save* them" (Acts 4:12).
- "Everyone who calls on the name of the Lord will be *saved*" (Acts 2:21, NIV).

## Saved . . . From What?

Have you ever heard someone's dramatic story of coming to know Christ and, in telling it, his old life almost sounds more appealing then the new one? He will describe in vivid detail all the adventures and exploits of sin and then, as sort of a P.S. say (yawn), "But now that I'm saved I read the Bible, go to church, and pray."

If this is the case, you are dealing with a person who does not really realize the significance of salvation, someone who does not understand what he or she has been saved *from*.

Do you really know how significant salvation is?

Do you realize what God has done for you?

Do you know how powerful and sufficient Jesus Christ and his salvation really are?

Okay, so what does it actually mean to be *saved*?

To be "saved" means you were in a serious, life-threatening situation. You were facing judgment and eternity in hell. But salvation, bought for you by the death of Jesus Christ on the cross in your place, has saved you from judgment and from hell. Romans 5:9-10 says,

> Since we have been *made right in God's sight* by the blood of Christ, he will certainly *save us from God's judgment.* For since we were re-stored to friendship with God by the death of his Son while we were still his enemies, we will certainly be delivered from eternal punishment by his life. [emphasis mine]

## Saved . . . For What?

Not only has Christ saved you from a future judg-ment, he is offering you abundant life. You don't need to live day by day as you were before you were saved, for now every day is filled with adventure for God.

Everything you need in life is found in a relation-ship with God! Paul wrote to the Colossians, "For in Christ the fullness of God lives in a human body, and you are complete through your union with Christ"

5

(Colossians 2:9-10). The word "complete" could be translated "to satisfy, to cram, finish, to fill up." In other words, through salvation, God is giving you more than you could ever fully utilize.

Often new believers (and sometimes older ones too) initially doubt that salvation has really come to them. The devil whispers, "Do you really think God would save someone like you? You psyched yourself into this. It's not real. You can trusssssssst me!"

This is nothing new.

Satan has been using this routine since the Garden of Eden, when he essentially said to Eve, "God did not say what you think he said."

Once you have trusted Jesus, you must realize that your salvation is not based on how you feel, but rather on what God has said.

Here are a few verses assuring you of your salvation.

- "All who believe in the Son of God know that this is true" (1 John 5:10).
- "For his Holy Spirit speaks to us deep in our hearts and tells us that we are God's children" (Romans 8:16).
- "I assure you, those who listen to my message and believe in God who sent me have eternal life. They will never be condemned for their sins, but they have already passed from death into life" (John 5:24).

- "I write this to you who believe in the Son of God, so that you may know you have eternal life" (1 John 5:13).

Notice that the last verse does not say "that you may *feel* that you have eternal life" or "that you may *hope* (if God is in a really good mood) that you have eternal life." It says, "That you may *know* you have eternal life."

You have been given the certainty of a new life, but that may mean some changes from how you used to live. But God also gives you a new power to live a new life. Romans 8:11-12 says, "The Spirit of God, who raised Jesus from the dead, lives in you. And just as he raised Christ from the dead, he will give life to your mortal body by this same Spirit living within you. So, dear brothers and sisters, you have no obligation whatsoever to do what your sinful nature urges you to do."

God wants to give you a complete and abundant life, but like light and darkness, God and sin will not coexist. You cannot continue in your old sinful ways and be pleasing to God. Your sin nature still exists, and you will sin at times, but your desires and attitudes need to change. This may mean making some drastic changes in order to let God's light shine into your life.

For the grace of God has been revealed, bringing salvation to all people. And we are instructed to turn from godless living and sinful pleasures. We should live in this evil world with self-control, right conduct, and devotion to God. . . . He gave his life to free us from every kind of sin, to cleanse us, and to make us his very own people, totally committed to doing what is right. (Titus 2:11-12, 14)

A truly saved person is "totally committed to doing what is right." Notice, you do not need to be a perfect person always doing what is right, but one who is committed to trying, by the grace of God, to change. When Christ lives in you, you are a different person! Paul wrote to the Corinthians, "What this means is that those who become Christians become new persons. They are not the same anymore, for the old life is gone. A new life has begun!" (2 Corinthians 5:17).

As a new believer, there simply must be changes in your life. Some people think that because they have "prayed to receive Christ," they can pretty much live as they please. They think they have taken care of heaven, so they can "live like hell." Some try to straddle these two worlds, but that just doesn't work. It's a lot like getting in the ocean when it's really cold. It's easier just to dive in or not get wet at all.

How do you know if you have truly become a Christian? What's going on in your heart? What do other people see in your attitudes and actions? God sees your heart, but people around you see how you're acting and if you're changing. James wrote,

"Now someone may argue, 'Some people have faith; others have good deeds.' I say, 'I can't see your faith if you don't have good deeds, but I will show you my faith through my good deeds.' Do you still think it's enough just to believe that there is one God? Well, even the demons believe this, and they tremble in terror! Fool! When will you ever learn that faith that does not result in good deeds is useless?" (James 2:18 20). Your faith must result in a changed life. Simply believing is not enough; actions will prove your faith.

Unfortunately, some want to claim to be believers but refuse to obey God's Word. Jesus made this searching statement about the Pretenders out there. "Not all people who sound religious are really godly. They may refer to me as 'Lord,' but they still won't enter the Kingdom of Heaven. The decisive issue is whether they obey my Father in heaven" (Matthew 7:21).

But what does this mean? It means if you are really saved, there will be clear results in your life. Works don't save anyone, but they are a good indication that you are saved. Some of these "works" will be discussed in the following chapters.

## A Spiritual Check-Up

Let's do a little "Spiritual Check-up" on our lives. Following are six indicators that you are living life as a new believer. (All of these come from the book of 1 John.)

9

## 1. You confessed Jesus Christ as Lord.

"All who proclaim that Jesus is the Son of God have God living in them, and they live in God" (1 John 4:15).

Obviously, this is important. You don't go anywhere without this first step. You accepted Jesus Christ. Now you need to tell someone else. You need to openly acknowledge that Jesus Christ is now your Lord and Savior.

## 2. You are seeking to obey Christ's commands.

"This is love for God: to obey his commands. And his commands are not burdensome, for everyone born of God overcomes the world. This is the victory that has overcome the world, even our faith" (1 John 5:3-4, NIV).

This is a problem for some people. They obey the commands they want to obey, the ones that don't conflict with the way they want to live. But Jesus said, "You are My friends if you do whatever I command you" (John 15:14, NKJV). You are to do *whatever* God commands—not whatever you personally agree with or whatever you find easy, but whatever he says.

Note also that verse 3 in 1 John says that "his commands are not burdensome." You will not find the Christian life to be miserable and confining. You will not discover that God is out to spoil all your fun. Instead, when you truly know Jesus, you will have a new outlook on life. You will have new God-given desires to please him, and you will want to avoid that which would displease him. Why? Because you love him. And because you love him, you will be seeking to obey his commands. You will not find them "burdensome." In fact, obedience will bring you the best joy possible!

### 3. You love and obey God's Word.

"But those who obey God's word really do love him. That is the way to know whether or not we live in him" (1 John 2:5).

In order to "obey God's word" you will have to read and study it. You will need to develop the habit of both Bible study and memorization, committing yourself to learning the Word of God. Sadly, many who have made commitments to Christ have never developed a good habit of Bible study. If you do not do that, you will be easy prey for the devil. The psalmist wrote, "I have hidden your word in my heart, that I might not sin against you" (Psalm 119:11). I still have permanently etched in my mind verses I committed to memory as a teenager (which was a long time ago!).

Paul gave these words to a young man named Timothy. "Do your best to present yourself to God as one approved, a workman who does not need to be ashamed and who correctly handles the word of truth" (2 Timothy 2:15, NIV). You will find a later chapter in this book that will help you learn how to get into God's Word. It is important that you learn to love the Bible, that it becomes a familiar book. God will speak to you through his Word. You will need to be listening.

### 4. You are miserable when you sin.

"No one who is born of God will continue to sin, because God's seed remains in him; he cannot go on sinning, because he has been born of God" (1 John 3:9, NIV).

The Greek translation of this verse would read, "Everyone who has been born of God does not habitually sin because his seed remains in him. And he is not able habitually to sin, because out of God he has been born."

Of course, this does not mean that you, as a Christian, will be sinless. But you should be sinning less and less. The Bible says that you need to repent of your sin. The word *repent* speaks of changing the direction in your life. This means when you really come to know Jesus Christ, you turn from all known sin. Only you can repent of your sin, and only God can forgive it.

Many have not taken this first, elementary step toward Christ. They say they have "received Christ," but they have not repented. In order to truly receive, you must also repent, because you must let go of one thing in order to take hold of another. If you commit a sin, and you feel miserable inside, then you can be sure that the Holy Spirit has taken up residence in your life and is doing some housecleaning!

## 5. You keep yourself out of Satan's way.

"We know that those who have become part of God's family do not make a practice of sinning, for God's Son holds them securely, and the evil one cannot get his hands on them" (1 John 5:18).

You are part of God's family and you are held securely, but you do need to protect yourself. Some people, places, and activities make it easier for the devil to tempt you. Now that you've been delivered from the kingdom of Satan, you have no desire to deliberately get back into his clutches. So you may need to change some ingrained patterns. Some friendships will change or end. Some recreational activities need to be replaced with something more wholesome. Remember, you're not giving up anything except what tears you down and seeks to destroy you. And you can replace all of those things with new friendships, new activities, and new desires and goals that will be better than you ever imagined!

## 6. You love other Christians.

"Everyone who believes that Jesus is the Christ is a child of God. And everyone who loves the Father loves his children, too" (1 John 5:1).

You might say, "Well, I haven't found a church I like yet, and besides, I work all week and Sunday is my only day off."

That's nothing more then a shallow excuse. You will find the time for what is important to you. And if you have truly been saved, gathering together with God's people for fellowship will be a priority in your life.

God says, "And let us not neglect our meeting together, as some people do, but encourage and warn each other" (Hebrews 10:25). He did *not* say, "Don't neglect meeting with other Christians unless Sunday is your only day off, in which case you are excused, because you just don't need fellowship as much as other Christians do."

So find a good church and attend regularly. Develop some Christian friendships. Seek out new relationships that will build you up in your faith.

As a new believer, you will find the above six earmarks showing up in your life. And people will notice. When they do, tell them what happened to you!

Will you slip up? Yes. Will you sin? Yes. Will you occasionally find yourself in an awkward situation because of this new faith that you're trying to work out in your life? Definitely. You have abandoned Satan's camp and joined his enemy—and he is now on the offensive to do what he can to bring you down.

I recently had the privilege of leading someone to the Lord. The thing that was holding him back from initially making that commitment was a fear of failing. I reassured him that God will give us the power to be the person he wants us to be. Being a Christian is not you trying to do it for God. Rather, it is Christ living in and through you. The Bible says, "Work out your salvation with fear and trembling" (Philippians 2:12, NIV). That does not mean that you have to somehow make your salvation happen. The verse could be translated, "With fear and trembling, carry to the goal and complete your own salvation." You will be moving step by step. Your eternity with Christ begins today. But you won't be walking alone, for the next verse continues: "For it is *God who works in you* to will and to act according to his good purpose" (Philippians 2:13, NIV, emphasis mine).

## Let's Get Moving!

As a new believer, you are a brand-new person. You may not look any different. You may only feel a little bit different. And you may not be sure where to go next. But rest assured, you have embarked on a lifetime with Christ that will cause you to have a life of such joy and fulfillment that you can hardly believe it.

What does your faith look like in your daily living? Read on, for this book will help you take those first few steps in your Christian life. Christ walks with you.

## HOW MY LIFE CAN CHANGE
## FOR THE BETTER

Niagara Falls has some great history. One of my favorite stories is about a tightrope walker named Jean Françoise Gravelet, known as "the Great Blondin." Trained in the European circus, he appeared at Niagara Falls and announced that he was going to cross the gorge on a tightrope.

On June 30, 1859, he made his first walk. During that walk, he stopped, lowered a rope to the Maid of the Mist, pulled up a bottle, sat down, and had a drink. Then, upon the final ascent to the other side, he stopped and did a backward somersault.

Other trips across the gorge would see him blindfolded, cooking an omelet, and even with his hands and feet manacled. He also pushed a wheelbarrow across. Before he began that particular stunt, the Great Blondin asked the gathered crowd, "Who thinks I can push this wheelbarrow across?"

The crowd shouted, "We believe!"

One man was shouting louder than all the others, "I believe you can!"

To which the Great Blondin replied, "Then get in!"

The man quickly disappeared!

Many people say, "I believe" when it comes to faith in Jesus Christ, but how many will actually get into God's "wheelbarrow"?

A flurry of recent survey research has found that, contrary to the secularism of popular culture, Americans believe in God and identify themselves as strongly religious. Nine out of ten say they have never doubted the existence of God. Ninety-six percent say that they believe in God.

But analysts who have studied the data say the spirituality of many Americans might be only skin-deep. Many claim to be "Christian" or at least "religious," but when it comes to climbing into God's wheelbarrow and going out over Niagara Falls on a tightrope—in other words, when their faith gets tested—they quickly disappear.

So what is true faith? The Bible says:

- We are saved by faith: "For it is by grace you have been saved, through faith—and this not from yourselves, it is the gift of God" (Ephesians 2:8, NIV).
- We are to live the Christian life by faith: "Now the just shall live by faith" (Hebrews 10:38, NKJV).
- Without faith, we cannot please God: "So, you see, it is impossible to please God without faith.

Anyone who wants to come to him must believe that there is a God and that he rewards those who sincerely seek him" (Hebrews 11:6).

## Saved by Faith

"It is by grace you have been saved, through faith" (Ephesians 2:8, NIV). It is important for you to know what true faith is and how you were saved by it. There is a phony kind of faith, a dead faith, that dramatically contrasts with the kind of faith God requires. Faith that produces no results or works cannot save anyone. It is simply an illusion. Jesus said, "Not all people who sound religious are really godly. They may refer to me as 'Lord,' but they still won't enter the Kingdom of Heaven. The decisive issue is whether they obey my Father in heaven" (Matthew 7:21).

The apostle James had a lot to say about faith. He discussed the importance of a faith that works when he wrote, "Dear brothers and sisters, what's the use of saying you have faith if you don't prove it by your actions? That kind of faith can't save anyone" (James 2:14).

Now don't misunderstand. James is not saying that *faith* can't save anyone—for we must have faith in order to be saved. He is saying that real faith, true faith, will produce change in a person's life. If a person's faith does not produce any change in his or her life, then it is not faith at all. Such faith is dead, unproductive, and shows no evidence of existence. Can that kind of faith save anyone? The answer—in a word—is no. Any declaration of faith that does not result in a changed life and good works is a false declaration.

This shows, of course, that there are many people who claim to have faith who really don't have it at all, at least not the kind of faith the Bible says we should have. And that is the only kind of faith that really matters, because that is the only kind of faith that will really save you eternally, and change you in this life.

The Scripture tells us that we are "justified by faith" (Romans 3:28, NIV). It is faith alone that justifies, but faith that justifies can never be alone. C. H. Spurgeon wrote, "Of what value is the grace I profess to receive if it does not dramatically change the way that I live? If it doesn't change the way that I live, it will never change my eternal destiny."

Clearly, faith is more than believing, for James goes on to say, "Do you still think it's enough just to believe that there is one God? Well, even the demons believe this, and they tremble in terror!" (James 2:19). It may surprise you to know that the demons and the devil himself believe in the existence of God, the deity of Jesus Christ, that the Bible is the very Word of God, and that Jesus is coming back again. The demons had great respect for and fear of Jesus Christ. James tells us that the demons believe and tremble. Why do they tremble? Because they believe not only in the person of Christ, but also in his power and authority. In fact, whenever they met Jesus while he was here on earth, they affirmed his authority. "Whenever the evil spirits saw him, they fell down before him and cried out, 'You are the Son of God'" (Mark 3:11, NIV). There is a recognition of his power over them, but their "faith" does not transform their character and conduct.

Another story is told of Simon the sorcerer, a man who appeared to believe but really did not. He lived in Samaria and had manipulated and misled people for some time. He had used demonic powers to lead the people into following him. Philip arrived in Samaria and began doing miracles by the hand of God, and Simon's followers turned from him and began to follow Philip. This was, needless to say, bad for Simon's business. Simon, seeing this, for all practical purposes "faked" a conversion.

This is not all that uncommon today. Sometimes a nonbelieving guy will say he is a Christian to get a Christian girl to go out with him. It seems to me that many politicians "get religious" around election time because they want the "evangelical vote." I'm more interested in the way they live the rest of the year, and yes, where they stand on issues that are important to me as a Christian.

Anyone can say he believes in Jesus. The proof, as they say, is in the pudding.

Simon the sorcerer needed to appear to be a believer so he could get his followers and his source of income back. So he was baptized as an indication of his newfound faith. The Bible says, "Then Simon

21

himself believed and was baptized. He began following Philip wherever he went, and he was amazed by the great miracles and signs Philip performed" (Acts 8:13). Peter and John arrived from Jerusalem to check out Philip's ministry, and through the laying of their hands on the believers, the Holy Spirit came. That's when Simon's true colors showed through.

"When Simon saw that the Holy Spirit was given when the apostles placed their hands upon people's heads, he offered money to buy this power. 'Let me have this power, too,' he exclaimed, 'so that when I lay my hands on people, they will receive the Holy Spirit!'" (Acts 8:18-19).

Peter, calling his bluff, told Simon to get his heart right with God. "Turn from your wickedness and pray to the Lord. Perhaps he will forgive your evil thoughts, for I can see that you are full of bitterness and held captive by sin" (Acts 8:22-23).

Put this all together with other passages in the Bible and it shows that, like the demons, people can believe in the power of God, believe that Jesus is the Son of God, believe that the Bible is his Word, and believe that Jesus is coming again. Like Simon, people can "believe" and be baptized. Yet those things, as important as they are, are not enough.

The point is, it's simply not enough to believe the right things. You must believe them *and* live them. True belief in Jesus Christ is the quality of faith that takes you to him to commit yourself to him, to rest completely upon him, to trust him fully. This will result in a radical change in your attitudes and lifestyle. But after you receive God's forgiveness through faith, that same faith should find expression in your life by how you live and behave.

## Living by Faith

"The just shall live by faith" (Hebrews 10:38, NKJV), meaning that since you have believed in Jesus and been made right with him by your faith, you should now live by that faith. Your faith and your works (meaning how you live your life) should go together like inhaling and exhaling. Faith is taking the gospel in; works is living the gospel out. You can't have one without the other. Like the two wings of an aircraft, both play their part.

The balance of faith and works is described in Ephesians 2:8-10 (NIV): "For it is by grace you have been saved, through faith—and this not from yourselves, it is the gift of God—not by works, so that no one can boast. For we are God's workmanship, created in Christ Jesus to do good works, which God prepared in advance for us to do." *Workmanship* is a word that describes a piece that is perfect. It comes from the Greek word *poiema*. We are God's work of art, his poem. How does this work of art, this poem, this thing of beauty express itself? Good works. God has a special work for you to do, a purpose to fulfill, a task to accomplish. Jesus said, "Let your good deeds shine out for all to see, so that everyone will praise your heavenly Father" (Matthew 5:16).

You may be asking, "Okay, so what are good deeds? What am I supposed to do?" I'm glad you asked. Here are just a few practical ways to "show your works" as a result of your faith.

### Faith Cares for Others

"Some people brought to [Jesus] a paralyzed man on a mat. Seeing their faith, Jesus said to the paralyzed man, 'Take heart, son! Your sins are forgiven'" (Matthew 9:2).

These men could have talked all day about the situation with their disabled friend; instead, they took direct action and they were rewarded.

The Bible says "But without faith it is impossible to please him, for he who comes to God must believe that he is, and that he is a rewarder of those who diligently seek him" (Hebrews 11:6, KJV). Clearly these four friends diligently sought Jesus, and they found their answer.

### Faith Obeys God's Commands

"Through him and for his name's sake, we received grace and apostleship to call people from among all the Gentiles to the obedience that comes from faith" (Romans 1:5, NIV).

We can talk all day long about how strong our faith is, but the bottom line is, we should put it to use—as in obedience. It's like having a tricked-out four-wheel drive SUV with all the latest off-road accessories. You've got the huge roll bar, the protective mesh screens over the headlights, the winch in the front, the huge tires, and the lift-kit. When someone suggests you do some off-roading, you shrink back in horror. "Are you crazy, do you know how much money I have in this thing? Besides, I just washed it!"

That's how a lot of people are with their faith: "All show and no go."

### Faith Trusts without Seeing

"We live by faith, not by sight" (2 Corinthians 5:7, NIV).

There will be times in your life as a Christian where God will allow you to go through times of trial and difficulty. It's not so hard to trust God when the sky is blue and the sun is out; it's another thing altogether when the storm clouds begin to gather. God wants us to learn to have faith in him even when we cannot feel or "see" him in our circumstances. This is called spiritual growth.

### Faith Reveals Christ

"Examine yourselves to see if your faith is really genuine. Test yourselves. If you cannot tell that Jesus Christ is among you, it means you have failed the test" (2 Corinthians 13:5).

There is nothing wrong with having a spiritual check-up every now and then. Just because you have done well for two months does not mean you're home free and will never mess up again. Spiritual growth is a constant process. The Christian life is like a greased pole—you are either climbing or slipping. Perhaps it's time for a "spiritual check-up" right now. Can people tell that Christ is in you?

### Faith Shows Love

"For when we place our faith in Christ Jesus, it makes no difference to God whether we are circumcised or not circumcised. What is important is faith expressing itself in love" (Galatians 5:6).

One of the most tangible results of having true, biblical faith is your attitude toward others—especially people you may have had some disdain for before your conversion.

Let me state this in the plainest terms. No follower of Jesus Christ should ever be bigoted toward others because of their socio-economic background, age, financial status, or race. We are commanded in Scripture to not only love other Christians, but indeed to love our very enemies (Matthew 5:44)!

### Faith Stands Firm

"Continue in your faith, established and firm, not moved from the hope held out in the gospel" (Colossians 1:23, NIV).

Faith will give you the root to stand when the storms of persecution and temptation come your way. And make no mistake about it, they *will* come. It's not a matter of *if*, but *when*. This is why you must "continue in your faith."

You cannot rest on your laurels. You must constantly be growing and learning spiritually. You must allow your roots to sink deeply into the soil of the teaching of Scripture, prayer, and active involvement in a church. This will help your faith to stand firm in times of trouble.

## Pleasing God by Faith

"It is impossible to please God without faith" (Hebrews 11:6). Do you want to please God? Do you want your life to change for the better? Then live by faith.

Now there has been some confusion among Christians when they consider faith and good works. James wrote, "So you see, we are made right with God by what we do, not by faith alone" (James 2:24), while Paul wrote, "So we are made right with God through faith and not by obeying the law" (Romans 3:28). So which is it—are we made right with God by our faith or by our good works?

Here's where it helps to understand the context of the author's comments. Paul was writing in response to the charge that believers had to perform all the intricacies of Moses' law from the Old Testament in order to be saved. Many Jews struggled with the fact that they still needed to follow all those regulations. While it is true that some parts of Moses' law are still to be followed (such as the Ten Commandments), many of the other parts (civil laws and regulations for sacrifices in worship) were for that time and place. So

Paul was making the point to his audience of Jewish Christians in Rome that they did not need to follow all of Moses' law in order to be saved. Faith in Christ's death was sufficient to bring them to God.

James, on the other hand, was writing to believers who had accepted that they had indeed been saved by their faith in Jesus Christ. These people, however, were in danger of resting in that fact, thinking that nothing further was required of them. Christ's death was so sufficient, they thought, that they could believe and then live any way they chose.

Faith justifies us before God, but works justify us before people. People cannot see our faith in God; only God can see that. All that people can see are the results in our lives. Jesus said, "Let your light so shine before men, that they may see your good works, and glorify your Father which is in heaven" (Matthew 5:16, KJV).

You must understand that you do not do "good works" in order to somehow continue to earn God's grace. Nor do you have to do these works in order to appease him or earn his blessing. The work of Christ on the cross satisfied all of God's righteous demands. But now you do good works because of what Christ has done for you and what the Holy Spirit is doing in you. Good works should flow from your life, not to earn or merit God's approval, but rather out of a recognition that you have already received it! When this happens, you have personally found the balance between faith and works about which Paul and James were writing.

Now there will be times when we fail to measure up to these standards, but God has made provision for that as well. The Bible says, "If we say that we have no sin, we deceive ourselves, and the truth is not in us. If we confess our sins, He is faithful and just to forgive us our sins and to cleanse us from all unrighteousness" (1 John 1:8-9, NKJV).

Perhaps as you have read this chapter, you have been doing a "spiritual check-up," and you realize that there are some areas that need to change. Good! Recognizing the problem is half the battle. Remember that "God is working in you, giving you the desire to obey him and the power to do what pleases him" (Philippians 2:13). The calling of God is the enabling of God. He will help you to be the person he wants you to be.

You have his word on it.

So get into God's wheelbarrow and let's go!

# Part Two

## JESUS IS MY FRIEND

*I no longer call you servants, because a master doesn't confide in his servants. Now you are my friends, since I have told you everything the Father told me.*

—JOHN 15:15

## 3

## GETTING TO KNOW HIM
## THROUGH BIBLE STUDY

Do you have any friends? Are you sure? How can you tell a real friend from a phony one? What makes for a true friendship?

I once heard the story of two friends who went camping in the woods. They woke up in the morning and were standing by their tent having their coffee when they suddenly spotted a huge grizzly bear heading for them at full speed. One man reached down and grabbed his running shoes and started putting them on. The other man looked at him and said, "What are you doing? Do you think you can outrun that grizzly bear?"

"No, and I don't need to," the first man answered. "I only need to outrun *you!*"

That's how a lot of so-called "friends" are. They run at the first sign of difficulty. It's been said that "a friend is one who walks in when others walk out." I wonder how many true friends you or I have. I wonder how good a friend you or I may be to someone else. I guess time will tell.

Many years ago, Socrates said, "Friend? There is no friend!" But Socrates did not know our Jesus, a true Friend who "sticks closer than a brother" (Proverbs 18:24). Without question, Jesus is the best friend you will ever have. Yes, you have become a believer and so you are Jesus' friend. You may have heard some Christians say, "Jesus is my best friend!" That may sound corny, but it's true. You can have a wonderful friendship with Jesus.

But what does that mean? How do you act out that friendship? When I was growing up, my family moved a lot. I was known more as "new kid" than by my real name. I did not always have a lot of steady friends. One of the good things that came out of that is I learned to think for myself at an early age and was not all that much influenced by peer pressure. The bad thing was that I didn't easily open up to people, being somewhat suspicious and standoffish. There are a few friends that I have today that I made years ago, but most of those earlier friendships are now long gone.

Occasionally someone comes up to me and tells me that he personally knows one of my "closest friends." When I ask the name of the person, nine times out of ten I have never even heard of him or her, much less had a close friendship with the person.

I think the Lord has a lot of friends like that, too. A lot of casual acquaintances (at best!) who don't have a real friendship with him. They could be called "fairweather" friends who will bail at the first mention of sacrifice or commitment.

So how do you become a close friend of Jesus? Like any friendship, your friendship with Christ is made up of two people committing themselves to each other. Friendship can only exist where there is mutual communication. Jesus demonstrated his willingness to be your friend by dying for you. The Bible says, "Here is how to measure it—the greatest love is shown when people lay down their lives for their friends" (John 15:13).

Clearly, Jesus has shown that he desires your friendship, for he laid down his life for you.

Many times when people want to share Christ with others, they quote Revelation 3:20, where Jesus tells us, "Behold, I stand at the door, and knock: if any man hear my voice, and open the door, I will come in to him, and will sup with him, and he with me" (KJV). The word *sup* simply means "have a meal." This is very significant. In Bible times the meal, especially dinner, was the main event of the day. It was a time of comfortably reclining on pillows around a low table and slowly eating, enjoying fellowship with others. It was a time to bare your heart, "let your hair down," discuss, and listen.

Jesus is saying to his church today that he wants his people to bare their hearts to him, to commune with him, and to listen to him.

Do you have this kind of friendship with God?

## Friends with Jesus

As noted above, friendship is a two-way street. In fact, Jesus went on to say, "You are My friends if you do whatever I command you" (John 15:14, NKJV). In these verses, Jesus pointed out five things about your friendship with him.

### True Friends of Jesus Obey Him

You can show your friendship with Jesus by doing what he says. If you don't, then you really have no right to call yourself his friend. As noted, the Lord said "You are My friends if you do whatever I *command* you."

For instance, a person may say he is your friend, even your close friend. But then you hear him talk about you behind your back, or you tell him a secret and he spreads it around, or he spreads outright lies about you. When you confront him, he admits it with a teary apology and, in his attempt to compensate for the wrongs he has done you, he may go out and buy you an expensive gift. Then he repeats the whole process again and again—hurting you, and then bringing you even more costly gifts to try to somehow make up for it. A pattern develops and you soon find that this becomes offensive.

After all, it's not his "stuff" you want, but his genuine and continual friendship.

In the same way, many people will fail the Lord on a constant basis and then try to compensate with some great act, like giving a large financial gift to the church. But God says, "Obedience is far better than sacrifice" (1 Samuel 15:22).

The Bible tells the story of King Saul, who was told to go and destroy the enemy and their livestock. Saul could not bring himself to completely obey the Lord; he decided to keep some of the loot and livestock for himself and his army. He didn't even acknowledge his disobedience. When confronted by the prophet Samuel, he lamely explained that the army had saved all the animals in order to sacrifice them to God.

Samuel was not impressed. More significantly, God was not impressed. Samuel explained that God wants obedience more than our sacrifices.

God wants you to obey him. After all he did for you, is this too much to ask?

### True Friends of Jesus Obey Actively

Some people think that it's enough simply to avoid what the Bible forbids. They might say, "I'm not a thief, an adulterer, or liar!" That would be like saying, "I am your friend because I do not rob you, insult you, or beat you up." Now although someone will certainly appreciate that you don't rob, insult, or injure him, he knows that those things alone don't make for friendship.

Friendship with Jesus is not just avoiding wrong things, but also doing right things. The Bible says, "Run from anything that stimulates youthful lust.

Follow anything that makes you want to do right. Pursue faith and love and peace, and enjoy the companionship of those who call on the Lord with pure hearts" (2 Timothy 2:22). You see, while you "run from" the bad stuff, you also need to "follow" and "pursue" the good stuff.

God wants you to be active in your obedience.

### *True Friends of Jesus Obey Continually*

As Jesus said, "You are My friends if you *do* whatever I command you." Jesus said to *do* what he commands. The word "do" in the verse is in a Greek form that means "continually." In other words, Jesus is talking about continuous obedience—not just once in a while on something big, not just when you feel like it—but always.

You might say, "It's impossible to obey perfectly all the time!" I know that. You need to understand that God knows you won't be able to do this perfectly. You will mess up—probably every day in some way. But the point is, you are trying to obey; you are seeking God's will; you are working on it.

When you fail, repent and try again! God's Holy Spirit has taken up residence in your life. The Bible says, "Be filled with the Spirit" (Ephesians 5:18). The verb "be filled" is in continuous tense, meaning, "Be constantly filled with the Spirit." While the Holy Spirit came into your life the moment you accepted Christ, you need to be "refilled" continually with the

Spirit's power. You will need to go to God daily for a fill-up. That will help give you the power for continual obedience.

### True Friends of Jesus Obey Even in the Smallest Matters

Again, Jesus says, "You are My friends if you do *whatever* I command you." Jesus said to do *what* he commands—not whatever you feel comfortable doing, or what you personally agree with, or what you find easy to obey. You are to obey what he says in his Word, not just in the big issues and decisions of life, but also in the little ones. Obedience in the small things makes it much easier to obey in the big things.

### True Friends of Jesus Obey Because They Want To

When you are in love with someone, you naturally want to do things that would please him or her. You buy a gift because you want to. You do things for the person because of your deep love, not out of fear of what he or she will do if you don't. Without question that is the highest motivator for serving God—doing what you do because you love him. The apostle Paul wrote, "Whatever we do, it is because Christ's love controls us" (2 Corinthians 5:14).

There is also a place for the fear of God in your service to him. But even that, for all practical purposes, is grounded in your love for him. Scripture says, "The fear of the LORD is the beginning of wisdom" (Psalm 111:10, NIV). The word *fear* could be interpreted as a

39

healthy dread of displeasing him. When you are Jesus' friend, you love and obey because you want to.

## Knowing God's Word

You know you need to obey, but the only way you'll know *what* to obey is to know God's Word, for the Lord reveals himself to us through Scripture. Jesus said, "Look, I have come to do your will, O God—just as it is written about me in the Scriptures" (Hebrews 10:7).

The Bible says, "All Scripture is inspired by God and is useful to teach us what is true and to make us realize what is wrong in our lives. It straightens us out and teaches us to do what is right. It is God's way of preparing us in every way, fully equipped for every good thing God wants us to do" (2 Timothy 3:16-17). In practical terms the Bible is your "User's Manual for the Christian Life." Everything you need to know about God and about living a life that pleases him are found in its pages. Look no further! In spite of the fact that false teachers periodically come along and say they have a "new" revelation from God, we need only look to God's Word for revelation. Why? Because if it's new, it's not true, and if it's true, it's not new.

In spite of the treasure-house that is in the Bible, it is tragic that so many believers go through life rarely opening its pages except on Sundays. Success or failure in the Christian life is determined by how much of the Bible you get into your heart and mind and how obedient you are to what you learn.

I heard the story of an old recluse who lived deep in the mountains of Colorado. When he died, some of his distant relatives came from the city to collect his valuables. Upon arriving, all they found was an old shack with an outhouse beside it. Inside the shack, next to the rock fireplace, they saw an old cooking pot and his mining equipment. A cracked table with a three-legged chair stood by a tiny window, an old kerosene lamp serving as its centerpiece. In the dark corner of the little room was a dilapidated cot with a threadbare bedroll on it. They picked up the old junk and left.

As they were driving away, an old, close friend of the recluse flagged them down.

"Y'all mind if I help myself to what's left in my friend's cabin?" he asked.

"Go right ahead," they replied. *After all,* they thought, *what inside that shack could be worth anything?*

The old friend entered the shack and walked directly over to the table. He reached under it and lifted up one of the floorboards. He then removed all the gold his friend had discovered in the previous 53 years—enough to have built a palace. Apparently the recluse had died with only his close friend knowing his true worth. As the friend looked out the little window and watched the cloud of dust behind the relatives' disappearing car, he said, "They shoulda got to know him better!"

The same is true with you and your friend Jesus Christ. Many people behave like distant relatives when Jesus invites them to intimate friendship. He has so many wonderful treasures to reveal to you from his Word. I was not raised in a Christian home. The Bible was unknown to me. When I asked the Lord to come into my life in my teens, I began to read it for the first time. I was amazed at how completely relevant it was to my life. At times I was surprised to find that the ink was dry on its pages, for it seemed as though it had been written just for me only moments before.

Why is it so important to study the Bible? The primary reason is because the Bible was inspired by God. It is, quite literally, his personal letter to you.

### The Bible Teaches You Truth

"All Scripture is inspired by God and is useful to teach us what is true." The Bible is the only book you need to discover the foundational truths of how to know and walk with God.

The Bible is your source of truth. As society changes, you don't need to flow with the currents of change. You can stand on the firm foundation of God's Word. You can know what's right and what's wrong.

The Bible is the source of theological truth—that is, the truth about God. There are lots of religions out there, some of which teach things that are totally opposed to what the Bible says. You need to read God's Word to know the truth and make sense of what you hear. At times, you might hear some weird, crazy ideas. The best thing is to know the Bible so well that when you hear something you can say, "No, that's not right because the Bible says this"; "That couldn't be true because the Bible says this"; or "That's exactly right because that's what Scripture says."

An inspector who worked for Scotland Yard in the counterfeit department was once asked if he spent a lot of time handling counterfeit money. He said no. He then explained that he spent so much time handling the real thing that he could immediately detect the counterfeit. Make no mistake—counterfeit "truth" is out there in force. As you become knowledgeable about God's Word, you will be able to detect teachings and concepts that are contrary to Scripture.

### The Bible Teaches You Right and Wrong

Read God's Word and he will show you when you're headed in the wrong direction. As you read and study God's Word, God will be working to mold you into the person he wants you to be. Only the inspired Word of God can be a personal letter to every believer who has ever lived. Martin Luther once said, "The Bible is alive. It speaks to me. It has feet. It runs after me. It has hands. It lays hold of me." Isn't that what you want? For God to speak to you and run after you and lay hold of you?

The Bible is more than just words on a page. Its words are alive. Through it, the Holy Spirit can speak to you personally. You're reading along and suddenly you sense Christ highlighting a key point or speaking to your sorrow or pain. The Bible is a key part of your personal conversation with God. As you get into the Word, God will speak to you.

### The Bible Guides You

"All Scripture . . . is God's way of preparing us in every way, fully equipped for every good thing God wants us to do" (2 Timothy 3:16-17). The greatest key to knowing God's will in almost any situation is knowing what his Word says. You need to learn to base your decisions on biblical principles as well as on the common sense God gave you—what God speaks to you personally, as well as what he speaks to you through those whom you respect.

I often wish that God would just speak to me audibly every morning and lay out my agenda for the day. But he doesn't. So how do I know God's will when I get up every morning? I read God's Word and then live out my day by faith based on biblical principles. When I come to a difficult situation or choice, I ask myself, *What biblical principles can guide me here? What does the Bible say?* Then I attempt to do that.

How does this happen? Reading the Bible will help you to develop "the mind of Christ." In other words, you'll read enough to eventually know, in essence, what Jesus would do in every situation. At times you will find exactly your answer. At other times, you will discover the Bible's basic principles regarding certain attitudes, actions, relationships, etc., and those will provide your answer. In any case, God will help you to know his will—in fact, he *wants* you to know his will. But he won't yell it at you from heaven; he'll show you as you seek him.

Paul wrote, "Don't let the world around you squeeze you into its own mold" (Romans 12.2, Phillips). The next phrase says, "Let God re-make you so that your whole attitude of mind is changed." This is the role of Scripture: to transform your mind as you immerse yourself in it.

## Studying God's Word

Here are some key questions you can ask yourself as you open the Bible and study a passage of Scripture:

- What is the main subject of the passage?
- Who are the people in this passage?
- Who is speaking?
- About whom is that person speaking?
- What is the key (most important) verse?
- What does this passage teach me about Jesus?

As you read, it is also very important to ask how the text might apply to your daily living. When reading a passage, ask yourself these questions:

- Is there any sin mentioned in the passage that I need to confess or forsake?
- Is there a command given that I should obey?
- Is there a promise made that I can look to in my current circumstances?
- Is there a prayer given that I could pray?

### *Meditating on His Word*

When you read the Bible, stop and think about what the Lord may be showing you. It's good to "chew" your spiritual food. That's what is meant by "meditating on the Word." Psalm 1 says the wise man "meditates day and night" on God's law (Psalm 1:2, NIV).

So even after you have read a passage, take time to ponder its meaning in your own life. You are better off reading five verses slowly and understanding what they mean than reading five chapters quickly and not getting anything out of them. Learn to slow down. Learn to meditate. Learn to allow the Holy Spirit to speak to you through each passage.

It is also important to pray before you start to read your Bible. Psalm 119:18 says, "Open my eyes to see the wonderful truths in your law." You need to come before the Lord and say something like "Father, I believe you are the author of this book. I believe, as you say in Scripture, that this book is breathed by you.

Therefore, I am asking you, as the author of the book, to take me on a guided tour. Help me to understand. Show me how these truths apply to my life." That form of sincere prayer will cause the Bible to come alive in your time of study.

### Treasuring His Word

Another principle of effective Bible study is found in Proverbs. You should turn your ear to wisdom; you should "look for it as for silver and search for it as for hidden treasure" (Proverbs 2:4, NIV). If you want to know God, he says that you should seek him and his wisdom as though you were mining for silver or searching for hidden treasures! Psalm 19:7 and 10 promise, "The law of the LORD is perfect, converting the soul: the testimony of the LORD is sure, making wise the simple. . . . More to be desired are they than gold, yea, than much fine gold: sweeter also than honey and the honeycomb" (KJV).

### Memorizing His Word

It is also very important to commit Scripture to memory. Many wonderful Bible memorization helps are available. Once Scripture is ingrained in your memory, it will always be there to use. There will be times when that verse or passage you memorized will pay great dividends. It will bring comfort to your heart, as well as needed strength in a time of intense temptation. We're told in Psalm 119:11, "I have hidden your word in my heart, that I might not sin against you." Although it is good to carry a Bible in your briefcase, pocket, or purse, the best place to carry it is in your heart!

In Deuteronomy 11:18-20, God tells us, "Commit yourselves completely to these words of mine. Tie them to your hands as a reminder, and wear them on your forehead. Teach them to your children. Talk about them. . . . Write them. . . ."

The best way for me to remember things is to write them down. When I write something down, it is engraved more deeply into my memory, much deeper than if I only read it. I might not even have to refer to what I wrote. Writing something down seems to help the material enter my mind and gives it more "staying power." It is a good practice to keep a journal or notebook with your Bible. When you study the Scripture and a passage speaks to you, write down what God has shown you. Maybe it won't be useful right at that moment, but the next day or a month later it may be just what you need.

### Receiving His Word

James says that believers should "humbly accept the message God has planted in your hearts, for it is strong enough to save your souls" (James 1:21). As you continue to read God's Word, it will take root and grow in your heart. Jesus used this same concept when he told a parable about a farmer who went out to plant seed. In those days, a farmer carried the seed in a bag and, as he walked, he tossed the seed. Jesus compared the human heart to the soil and God's Word to the seed. In this story, Jesus described four kinds of soil that pictured four kinds of hearts:

- The hard heart, which did not understand or receive the Word; therefore, the Word could not take root and grow;
- The shallow heart, which was very emotional but had no depth and bore no fruit;
- The crowded heart, which lacked repentance and permitted sin to crowd out the Word;
- The fruitful heart, which received the Word and allowed it to take root, grow to maturity, and bear fruit.

You determine what kind of soil your heart will be. It all comes down not only to hearing God's Word, but to obeying it. The Word of God cannot work in your life unless you receive it in the right way. It's possible to hear with your ears but not with your heart.

Studying God's Word should always lead to obedience, a changed life, and a changed attitude.

So dig in and start the adventure of knowing God through his Word!

## GETTING TO KNOW HIM
## THROUGH PRAYER

I heard the story of three ministers debating the best posture for prayer. As they were talking, a telephone repairman was working on the phone system in the background.

One minister shared that he felt the key was in the hands. He always held his hands together and pointed them upward as a symbolic form of worship. The second suggested that real prayer was conducted on one's knees. The third suggested that they both were wrong—the only position for prayer was flat on one's face.

By this time, the telephone repairman couldn't stay out of the conversation any longer. He blurted out, "I have found that the most powerful prayer I ever made was while I was dangling upside down by my heels from a power pole, suspended forty feet above the ground!"

Have you ever been in a situation like that? Perhaps you felt as if your life was hanging by a thread. Or maybe troubles just came crashing in on you in rapid succession. What should you do? Well, my advice is, you should pray!

## What Is Prayer, Anyway?

Put simply, prayer is communication with God. Before you became a believer, you may have said a prayer at a meal or bedtime or, like the telephone repairman, in the middle of a crisis in your life. Now that you are a believer, prayer is your lifeline, your subsistence. It should become as second nature to you as breathing. It s hould infuse every part of your life.

You may be intimidated about the very thought of talking to God. Perhaps you think he's just too big to want to deal with your little problems. But that's where you're wrong. God wanted a relationship with you—so much so that he gave his Son to die for you. Now he desires intimacy and closeness with you, and the only way to do that is through regular communication with him.

So what do you talk to God about? Well, everything. You can wake up talking to him, asking his guidance throughout the day, sending up a quick prayer for patience at a moment of need, and simply conversing with God as your ever-present friend.

Of course, you should also set aside times of prayer when you can talk to God at length and listen to him in silence. Jesus did this as well: "The next morning Jesus awoke long before daybreak and went out alone into the wilderness to pray" (Mark 1:35).

Luke also tells us that "Jesus often withdrew to the wilderness for prayer" (Luke 5:16).

The Bible tells us that the Holy Spirit helps us when we pray. The moment you asked Jesus to be your personal Lord and Savior, you were sealed by the Holy Spirit. One of the many things he does is help you in prayer—especially at those times when you don't know what to pray. "And the Holy Spirit helps us in our distress. For we don't even know what we should pray for, nor how we should pray. But the Holy Spirit prays for us with groanings that cannot be expressed in words. And the Father who knows all hearts knows what the Spirit is saying, for the Spirit pleads for us believers in harmony with God's own will" (Romans 8:26-27). As you realize how intimately God is involved in your prayers, you will begin to feel a unique closeness to him.

## Why You Should Pray

The constant communication with God keeps you going and growing in your Christian life. Just as your marriage will face difficulty if you and your spouse never talk to each other—or only talk during times of crisis—so your relationship with God will stagnate without communication.

Some people think, "Why should I pray if God already knows everything?" While it is true that God is all-knowing and that he knows your needs even before you ask him, he still wants you to communicate with him, to verbalize your needs to him, to show your faith by your request.

### Talk to God about Needs and Requests

You should not demand things from God as though he were some "cosmic butler" prepared to answer your every whim. Yet it is also wrong to refuse to bring your needs to him. God *wants* you to ask him to bless your life, meet your needs, and spiritually strengthen you. God wants to bless you because you are his child. Unfortunately, many believers fail to receive what God has for them because they don't pray. James wrote, "The reason you don't have what you want is that you don't ask God for it" (James 4:2). There is such a thing as a sin of omission, meaning that we don't do what we ought to do. Clearly, failing to pray falls in that category. Jesus reproved Peter for failing in this regard, and it ultimately led to his spiritual downfall (Matthew 26:40-41).

Whatever need you are facing today, whatever concern is heavy on your heart, whatever worry is plaguing you, whatever guidance you need—God wants to hear about it. He wants you to bring it to him. The writer to the Hebrews put it this way: "So let us come boldly to the throne of our gracious God. There we will receive his mercy, and we will find grace to help us when we need it" (Hebrews 4:16). You can go boldly to the throne of your gracious God through prayer.

The Bible reminds us, "Don't worry about anything; instead, pray about everything. Tell God what you need, and thank him for all he has done. If you do this, you will experience God's peace, which is far more wonderful than the human mind can understand. His peace will guard your hearts and minds as you live in Christ Jesus" (Philippians 4:6-7).

## Ask For Forgiveness

There will be many times when you will sin, you'll realize it, and you'll need to talk to God about it. You may find yourself weighed down by guilt over something that you know displeases God. If so, good! That's means God is at work in your life, working to make you more like Christ. Just as your body has a warning system called pain that alerts you to danger, your soul has a warning system called a conscience. A guilty conscience signals that something in your heart needs to be confronted and cleansed to keep your relationship with God from suffering.

So what do you do about sin? First of all, you need to realize that what you did was indeed a sin—you need to call it what it is. Don't blame it on someone or something else. Take personal responsibility for it and, as the Bible says, "repent" of it. The word *repent* means to change your direction. It's not enough merely to feel sorry for sin (although that is important). You need to change. Besides, if it's real sorrow, you will *want* to turn from that sin.

The Bible tells us, "For God can use sorrow in our

lives to help us turn away from sin and seek salvation. We will never regret that kind of sorrow. But sorrow without repentance is the kind that results in death" (2 Corinthians 7:10).

You do that through prayer. In your conversation with God, you acknowledge that what you did was wrong, you ask forgiveness, ask God to help you in the future, and commit yourself to turn to him when you face trouble and temptation in the future. The Bible promises, "If we confess our sins to him, he is faithful and just to forgive us and to cleanse us from every wrong" (1 John 1:9).

### Overcome Worry

Prayer also can help you to stop worrying. When you get down to it, worry is a completely worthless exercise. It's a lot like sitting in a rocking chair. You are moving, but you're not going anywhere.

I heard the story of a man who was known to be given over to excessive worry day in and day out. He looked like he was carrying the weight of the world on his bent-over shoulders. Then one day his friends noticed a smile on his face and a spring in his step. They said, "You look different! What's happened to you?"

"I don't worry about anything anymore!" he exclaimed.

One of his friends said to him, "Why, you're the biggest worrywart on the planet! How did you suddenly stop worrying about things?"

The former worrywart responded, "I took an ad out in the paper offering $1000 a day if someone would do my worrying for me. Some guy responded, and now he does just that!"

"One thousand bucks a day?" the friend gasped. "You don't make that kind of money! How are you going to pay this guy?"

The former worrywart responded, "That's for him to worry about!"

But better than hiring someone to worry for you, you might want to pray about these things instead. So how can you stop worrying? The answer is given in the Bible. Again quoting from Philippians, "Don't worry about anything; instead, pray about everything. Tell God what you need, and thank him for all he has done. If you do this, you will experience God's peace, which is far more wonderful than the human mind can understand. His peace will guard your hearts and minds as you live in Christ Jesus" (Philippians 4:6-7).

God wants to be the first one you turn to in times of worry or crisis. Don't ever think that your concern is too insignificant for God. He said, "Pray about everything." That means *everything!*

The next time you are tempted to worry about something, take the time and energy you would spend worrying and channel them into prayer. You can say something like, "Lord, here is my problem. It seems so big, and I can't deal with it. I'm worried about what to do, how it will turn out, how to handle it. So I am going to stop worrying and give this problem to you. I'm going to put it in your hands and trust you to help me deal with it." When you do that, you will receive "God's peace," a peace that will guard your heart and mind.

## *Increase Spiritual Knowledge and Maturity*

This is the nitty-gritty of communication with God. Too often people don't seek God's guidance until after they make a critical decision. God wants his people to come to him *first,* so he can guide and direct them. Thus you need to call upon God—and you do that through prayer.

But communication is a two-way street. You not only talk to God, but you also *listen.* God says that when we call upon him, he will answer us. The psalmist, referring to those who love the Lord, wrote God's words: "When they call on me, I will answer; I will be with them in trouble. I will rescue them and honor them" (Psalm 91:15). Jesus also told his followers, "Ask and it will be given to you; seek and you will find; knock and the door will be opened to you" (Matthew 7:7, NIV).

How do you know when God is answering? Well, you need to be attentive, actively listening for God's answer. One way is to study the Bible. God has given you a wealth of spiritual knowledge and wisdom in his Word. Studying the Bible gives the Holy Spirit an opportunity to help you understand God's Word and how it applies to specific situations in your life. You can also pay attention to circumstances that surround your prayer requests. How are they changing—or not changing—in light of your prayers? God's answers may sometimes be found in the outcome of these situations.

If you want to be a growing and maturing Christian, you must seek God and his guidance daily. The more you commune with God, the more you will begin to see God at work in you.

Here is something that may surprise you: God wants to speak to you even more than you want to hear him speak. He wants to bless you even more than you want to be blessed. God delights in blessing his children. And that includes giving you his guidance and direction through prayer.

James reminds us, "If you need wisdom—if you want to know what God wants you to do—ask him, and he will gladly tell you. He will not resent your asking. But when you ask him, be sure that you really expect him to answer, for a doubtful mind is as unsettled as a wave of the sea that is driven and tossed by the wind" (James 1:5-6).

## How You Should Pray

Okay, how do you go about this thing called "praying"? What do you do? Well, unlike the conversation among the ministers at the beginning of this chapter, there is no special position you need to be in, no special way you have to hold your hands, no special

59

words you have to say. You don't need to talk in "thees" and "thous" as though God is still stuck in King James's England. You start communicating with God. That's prayer.

Beyond that, however, let me give you some advice on how to pray.

### Pray First

You need to get into the habit of going to God right away with everything that comes into your life. When it's good, say, "Thanks!" When it isn't, say, "Help!" Too often Christians exhaust every other means of solving a problem and then decide to try God as a last resort. Instead, go to God first. Now, his answer may indeed include lots of things he'll want you to do (in other words, he won't always drop the answer you want from the sky), but then you can proceed knowing you are right in the center of his will.

### Pray Regularly

The Bible tells us to "pray without ceasing" (1 Thessalonians 5:17, KJV). That doesn't mean, of course, that you must give up eating, sleeping, and working. The point is that you constantly have an attitude of prayer—the line is connected and you can pray at a moment's notice.

For example, think about times when you have been stuck on the freeway. Did you know that is a great time to pray? (Keep your eyes open, of course!) You can pray anytime, anywhere, in any position. The main thing is that you pray. Jesus said that we should always pray and not give up or lose heart (Luke 18:1).

How wonderful it will be when you take a request to God and almost immediately see it answered miraculously! You will experience such a great thrill to know that almighty God has been listening to you!

However, not all your prayers will be answered that way. You must remember that God is not on a human timetable. So when you pray and *don't see* an answer, don't give up. If God seems to be telling you that the request is inappropriate or not in line with his will, then you should stop praying. But you may know that the request is in line with his will, but he just isn't giving the answer you want at the time you want. That is not unusual. Keep on praying. It's okay to be persistent in prayer. In fact, Jesus told a parable to show that his followers should never stop praying (see Luke 18:1-8). When the time is right according to God, then he will answer.

Sometimes God says "Slow," sometimes God says "Go," sometimes God says "No," and sometimes God says, "Grow."

For instance, you may have the right idea, but your timing is off. You are praying for the Lord to bring you a mate or to open up a ministry opportunity. God's answer to you is "Slow."

Then there are times when you ask for something and before you even finish the prayer the Lord has said yes or "Go!"

Then there are other times when the thing you are praying for is clearly out of the will of God and the Lord says, "No." It's interesting that often when people hear a no from heaven, they say, "God did not answer my prayer!" But the fact of the matter is that *no* is as much of an answer as *yes*. And God may simply give a no answer even to a good request—remember, he's in charge.

Finally, there are those times when the Lord will say, "Grow." In other words, he has a thing or two he wants to teach you through this situation you're praying about. For example, the apostle Paul had a particular physical problem, some kind of illness or affliction that he asked God to heal. He prayed persistently and with faith, but the Lord did not do what he had asked. Paul wrote this about it: "Three different times I begged the Lord to take it away. Each time he said, 'My gracious favor is all you need. My power works best in your weakness.' So now I am glad to boast about my weaknesses, so that the power of Christ may work through me" (2 Corinthians 12:8-9). Essentially, God was telling Paul to "Grow." There were certain lessons the apostle would learn in this situation that he would not learn otherwise.

### Pray Expectantly

When you pray, be ready! God will indeed answer. Sometimes you will get a yes, sometimes a no, sometimes a wait—but you always will get an answer.

"And we can be confident that he will listen to us whenever we ask him for anything in line with his will. And if we know he is listening when we make our requests, we can be sure that he will give us what we ask for" (1 John 5:14-15).

What a great promise! You must understand, however, that prayer is not about getting what you want; it's about getting what *God* wants. Prayer is not an argument with God in which you try to persuade him to do things for you; instead, prayer is an exercise in which God's Spirit enables you to know and ask for things in line with his will. True prayer is not about getting your will in heaven; it's about getting God's will on earth.

Everyone likes to quote the part of the above verse that says God will give you what you ask for; but you must remember that you are to be asking "in line with his will." Without a doubt, God will answer those requests with a resounding yes. So the key to having your prayers answered in the affirmative is to discover the will of God. The primary way of doing that is through careful study of the Scriptures. Jesus said, "Look, I have come to do your will, O God—just as it is written about me in the Scriptures" (Hebrews 10:7). Jesus will come to you and reveal his will for you through "his book," the Bible.

## When You Should Pray

Of course, you are to be praying anytime about anything. It can be an interesting study, however, to look into the Bible and see some of the practical instances of prayer.

In the book of James, several verses give three specific and practical areas in which prayer is important:

- When you're afflicted (James 5:13)
- When you're sick (James 5:14-15)
- When specific needs occur in your life (James 5:16-18)

### Times of Affliction

Let's consider times of affliction, trouble, or difficulty. James wrote, "Are any among you suffering? They should keep on praying about it" (James 5:13). The word "suffering" could be translated "trouble" or "distress." What should you do as a believer when you find yourself in trying circumstances? The temptation may be to blame and strike out at others. Some people even become angry at the Lord for allowing the trouble in the first place. Others prefer the option of self-pity. James says, however, to pray!

That is because prayer can remove affliction, if it is God's will. But prayer can also give you the grace you need to endure your troubles and be brought much closer to God in the process (as we saw in the case of the apostle Paul).

Consider praying for wisdom so that you can know if your troubles are just part of your circumstances or if they have been brought on by your disobedience to God. Earlier in his letter, James says, "If any of you lacks wisdom, let him ask of God, who gives to all liberally and without reproach, and it will be given to him" (James 1:5, NKJV).

If you have brought on your own troubles, you are simply facing the consequences of your own disobedience. Like Jonah who was swallowed by the great fish because he tried to run from God, you may also have to repent from inside your difficulty! God will not necessarily change the consequences (although there are times when he will graciously do even that), but he *will* be with you to guide you and help you. So keep on praying!

But maybe, like Job, the troubles have come upon you through no disobedience or sin. The fact of the matter is, you were walking very closely with God. All of Job's afflictions came on him as a result of attacks by Satan that were allowed by God. Satan may have sent the affliction you are presently experiencing to try to weaken your faith. God promises to go with you through it. So keep on praying!

The Bible tells the story of Paul and Silas being thrown into prison for preaching the gospel. They were whipped, their legs were put in stocks, and they sat in a dark and dank prison. What do you think they did? They didn't question God, become angry at him, or beg to be released. Instead, "around midnight, Paul and Silas were praying and singing hymns to God, and the other prisoners were listening" (Acts 16:25). No groans or complaints were coming from their mouths; instead, they prayed and sang!

When you are in pain, the darkness seems like midnight, and the last thing you want to do is sing. But God promises to bring you joy. Even in the darkness, he promises "songs in the night" (Job 35:10).

In times of affliction, you need to pray like Jesus, "O My Father, if it is possible, let this cup pass from Me; nevertheless, not as I will, but as You will" (Matthew 26:39, NKJV).

In times of trouble, pray, keep on praying, and trust in God.

### Times of Sickness

When we are sick, we should pray, too. James 5:14-15 says, "Are any among you sick? They should call for the elders of the church and have them pray over them, anointing them with oil in the name of the Lord. And their prayer offered in faith will heal the sick, and the Lord will make them well. And anyone who has committed sins will be forgiven."

Here we are given the scriptural pattern for healing. As believers, we lay hold of the promise of physical healing. Oil was used in the Old Testament as a symbol of supernatural anointing. David was anointed with oil by the prophet Samuel as a sign that David had been chosen by God to be the next king of Israel. Oil is also a symbol of the Holy Spirit.

When you or someone you know is sick, you can

ask the leaders of the church for prayer. Nowhere in the Bible do we read of "faith healers" or people who have a "healing ministry." Miracles and healings were not the focus; the focus was the proclamation of the Word of God. So you don't need to seek out some great "healer" to receive a touch from God. You are simply to pray and ask others to pray for you and with you. James also adds that it is especially important to ask the leadership of your church to pray for you.

The words "their prayer offered in faith will heal the sick" is not a blanket promise that every sick person will be healed. Even the great apostle Paul did not see everyone for whom he prayed healed. He wrote to Timothy that he "left Trophimus sick in Miletus" (2 Timothy 4:20). I already mentioned that Paul himself had some kind of physical affliction that God refused to heal (2 Corinthians 12:7-10). Clearly, God is sovereign and will heal whomever he chooses. We must ask in faith, trusting that God will do what is best.

### Times of Need

Your prayers are powerful; there is no doubt about that. James 5:16 says, "The earnest prayer of a righteous person has great power and wonderful results."

You might think, "Well, I'm not righteous, so this verse doesn't apply to me." Yet the Bible tells you that you really *are* righteous before God. "God will also declare us to be righteous if we believe in God, who brought Jesus our Lord back from the dead" (Romans 4:24). So you see, you have been declared righteous by God. So when you pray, your prayers will have great power and wonderful results!

James gives an example of a time when powerful prayer met a specific need: "Elijah was as human as we are, and yet when he prayed earnestly that no rain would fall, none fell for the next three and a half years! Then he prayed for rain, and down it poured. The grass turned green, and the crops began to grow again' (James 5:17-18). Elijah was a prophet who was known for special acts of courage and dramatic miracles. God worked through him. Elijah brought the word of the Lord to the disobedient leaders in Israel. He had already told them no rain would fall (1 Kings 17:1); then several years later, he prayed for rain and it immediately rained (1 Kings 18:41-45).

He was God's spokesman, but he also prayed with earnestness. When he went to Mount Carmel to pray for rain, he really put his heart into it. It was not a laid-back request, but a passionate prayer during which he "fell to the ground" (1 Kings 18:42).

You are a righteous person before God, but do you pray earnestly, intensely, with your whole heart? You'll be amazed at the power of your prayers!

Are you in trouble or distress? Pray!
Are you sick? Pray!
Are you in need? Pray!

It's true—sometimes things can look pretty bleak, but keep on praying! See what God will do in response to your faithful, earnest, trusting prayers.

## God's Part, Your Part

I want to close this chapter with an important distinction. Yes, there is a place for miracles, but there is also a place for our own efforts. Sometimes we think we should just sit back and pray, and in response, God will do everything. But we do not necessarily see that pattern in Scripture.

The Bible tells the story of Jesus coming to the tomb of Lazarus who had died. The process of decomposition had already begun. Jesus stood at the tomb of his departed friend and shouted, "Lazarus come forth!" (John 11:43, KJV). And sure enough, Lazarus came back to life.

Now that was God's part.

Only Jesus could do that.

But there was something for others to do as well.

The Bible tells us, "And Lazarus came out, bound in graveclothes, his face wrapped in a headcloth. Jesus told them, 'Unwrap him and let him go!'" (John 11:44). You see, only Jesus could raise Lazarus from the dead, but someone else had to loose him from his graveclothes.

Then there is the story of the feeding of the five thousand. A huge multitude had gathered to hear the Lord's words. As mealtime approached, the people were hungry. There was a young boy there who had a few loaves of bread and some fish. Jesus took what this young man had, miraculously multiplied it, and fed the crowd (John 6:1-13).

It is interesting to note, however, how Jesus involved his followers in the process. "Then Jesus took the loaves, gave thanks to God, and passed them out to the people. Afterward he did the same with the fish. And they all ate until they were full. 'Now gather the leftovers,' Jesus told his disciples, 'so that nothing is wasted'" (John 6:11-12). Only Jesus could multiply five loaves and two fish to feed five thousand people, but someone had to distribute the food and pick up the leftovers.

Sometimes people ask God for miracles when God just wants them to take practical steps. Let's say you have a job, but you don't want to go to work this week because you're not in the mood. You'd rather stay home and watch television. So you don't work all week long. You call in sick every day even though you're feeling fine. Then at the end of the week you don't get a paycheck. As a result, you become hungry. So you begin to pray, "Oh God, send me food. Oh Lord, I know you can do it. Lord, you provided for Elijah and I just pray that you'll provide for me too. I have faith that you can do it!"

But no food comes. Why not? Because you don't need a miracle; you need to get back to work! You're praying for a miracle, but you're violating biblical principles in the process. The Scripture teaches, "Whoever does not work should not eat" (2 Thessalonians 3:10). If you have the ability and the opportunity to work and you don't do so because you just don't feel like it, it's your own fault when you don't receive the material things you need.

On the other hand, sometimes we try to do what only God can do. Suppose you pray for an unsaved friend to come to Christ. But then you think, *God needs my help. Some high-pressure witnessing tactics should do the job.* So you start badgering your friend to repent and believe, thinking God can't save him without your "help."

The result? You end up complicating things. Do your part by being a loving, caring friend, sharing the gospel when God provides the opportunity, inviting your friend to church, and praying fervently. Then allow God to do what only he can do.

May God help you to learn how to pray. It will be an exciting adventure for you to see all that the Lord will do for, in, and through you through prayer.

The Lord longs to hear from you. His line is never busy. He is never preoccupied. He wants to hear your prayer. So pray!

# 5

## GETTING TO KNOW HIM THROUGH FELLOWSHIP WITH OTHER BELIEVERS

While it is extremely important that you grow in your personal walk with Christ through Bible study (see chapter 3) and prayer (see chapter 4), you cannot go it all alone. You need fellowship with other believers. To do that, you need to look for and regularly attend a church.

Some people think they can get enough spiritual input from Christian television, radio, or books. Or perhaps they think they can worship outside in nature better than inside a church building. While all of those activities have their place, nothing can substitute for involvement in a local body of believers—a church.

The word *church* can refer to all the Christians across the entire world, for we are all united in what we call "the body of Christ." You became a part of that "church," that "body of believers" when you accepted Christ.

Thus you need to find a "church home," a place

where you will be fed from God's Word and given spiritual instruction, where you can worship and pray with other believers, and where you will be able to serve with the gifts and abilities God has given you. It simply is not an option but a true spiritual necessity, that is, if you want to grow spiritually.

## Why Go to Church?

Why is the church so important? Well, because the church is the only organization that Jesus himself established. To his disciple Peter, he said, "Now I say to you that you are Peter, and upon this rock I will build my church, and all the powers of hell will not conquer it" (Matthew 16:18). Clearly the church was an "of course" to Jesus, and it should be an "of course" to every believer.

Regular involvement in a church and fellowship with other believers are vital building blocks to your Christian faith. As you go into a church and find your place in it, you can then give to others what God has given to you. Your talents, given to you by God, can be used in the church to serve God and build his kingdom. A healthy church will be filled with people who not only listen and learn, but also are involved and serve. The people do not come to the church looking only to be cared for and blessed (although that should happen!), they should also come desiring to help and to use their gifts to serve the Lord and his people.

The Bible says, "And let us not neglect our meeting

together, as some people do, but encourage and warn each other, especially now that the day of his coming back again is drawing near" (Hebrews 10:25). For you as a new believer, interaction with other believers is very important. This means that taking this time every week should be a major priority in your life as a follower of Jesus.

Some people will say, "But I work all week and Sunday is my only day off!" But note that Hebrews 10:25 does *not* say, "And let us not neglect our meeting together, *unless of course Sunday is your only day off, in which case you are excused because you don't need fellowship as much as other Christians do.*"

No, Scripture tells us not to stop our meeting together. You need the church. The church needs you. Without the church, you will not grow as you ought to spiritually.

But why is the church so important?

First, involvement in a healthy church will *provide you with encouragement and love.* You need a place where you can be encouraged in your faith and reminded that you are a member in God's family. At church, you are surrounded by people who also love Christ. You will have a sense of belonging and acceptance that you won't find any longer out in the world.

Second, involvement in a healthy church will *allow you to learn from more mature Christians.* Many believers in the church have been walking with Christ for many years, through many life situations. You can learn from these people and gain spiritual wisdom and insight for your personal walk with Christ. They can "take you under their wing" and help you see how mature followers of Jesus live and think. That is called "discipling." Then when you get stronger spiritually, you can do the same for someone else.

Third, involvement in a healthy church will *help you to discern the truth and so avoid wrong teaching.* You hear lots of messages from all kinds of sources, but your continued growth as part of a healthy church will help you to be able to know the truth and spot the error.

Finally, involvement in a healthy church will *prepare you for Christ's return.* All believers are awaiting that day. Whether or not it comes in your lifetime, you want to be living for Christ every day, preparing yourself to one day live with him. Believers also need to encourage one another through difficult times.

The church needs you! It needs your involvement, your gifts, your encouragement, your faith. So the next step is to find where God wants you.

## How to Find a Church

In fact, the first believers in Jerusalem immediately became a "church." After Peter delivered a sermon to the Jews who were in Jerusalem for a special festival, many believed. The Bible tells us that "those who believed what Peter said were baptized and added to the church—about three thousand in all" (Acts 2:41).

Notice that they were "added to the church." That was the first group of believers. The next verse tells us what this "church" was doing: "They joined with the other believers and devoted themselves to the apostles' teaching and fellowship, sharing in the Lord's Supper and in prayer. . . . And each day the Lord added to their group those who were being saved" (Acts 2:42, 47).

Acts 2 is about the birth of the church. In fact, it is about the first day in the life of the church. This church lacked every worldly advantage; it was attacked both spiritually and physically, but it not only survived, it flourished! As Jesus had said, "all the powers of hell" could not defeat it (Matthew 16:18).

You've probably noticed that there are a lot of churches out there today. You can easily be overwhelmed and wonder how to find the right one for you. Where do you begin?

First of all, of course, you pray. Ask God to guide you to the place where he would have you attend, serve, and grow. Beyond that, there are four things that stand out in Acts 2:42 about the church that Jesus founded, and these can be helpful to you as you begin your search for a church:

1. It was a learning church.
2. It was a loving church.
3. It was a worshiping church.
4. It was an evangelistic church.

## A Learning Church

We are told that the believers in the first church "devoted themselves to the apostles' teaching." The King James translation of this verse says "the apostles' doctrine," meaning their teaching about the fundamental tenets or cornerstones of Christianity. Clearly, that was what the apostles were teaching—the basics of this brand-new faith.

Notice that in the first church, the believers "devoted themselves" to learning the apostles' teachings about doctrine. These people were devoted to learning, hungry to discover more. This was not a casual attitude as one might have joining a social club. There seems to be a spiritual excitement in what they did. They applied themselves to what was being taught from the Word.

As a new believer, you need to find a church that teaches clear Bible doctrine. This simply means that you need to be instructed in the basics of the Christian faith. It could be compared to building a house. When you build a house, you don't start with the wallpapering or the landscaping. You start with a good foundation. Otherwise everything else is rather meaningless. In the same way, when you are building your spiritual life, you need a good foundation. And that will happen in a church that teaches you the Word of God, line by line, book by book, so you can understand all that God says in his Word.

Some well-meaning but misguided person might

say something like, "Oh, I'm not into doctrine. I just want to love Jesus!" The problem with that kind of thinking is if you don't have a good foundation in Bible doctrine and theology, you might end up loving "the wrong Jesus!"

C. S. Lewis gave this warning years ago, in his book *Mere Christianity*: "If you do not listen to Theology, that will not mean that you have no ideas about God. It will mean that you have a lot of wrong ones—bad, muddled, out-of-date ideas."

Some Christians think that they don't have to use their intellect. But that's wrong. If you really want to know Jesus and grow in your love for him, you need to study doctrine. And where is doctrine found? In the pages of Scripture! "All Scripture is inspired by God and is useful to teach us what is true and to make us realize what is wrong in our lives. It straightens us out and teaches us to do what is right. It is God's way of preparing us in every way, fully equipped for every good thing God wants us to do" (2 Timothy 3:16-17).

Look for a church that places a high priority on Bible study. Studying the Bible is important to every Christian's spiritual growth. Without Bible study, Christians cannot know and understand God's commands and truth. A healthy, learning church is where the Spirit of God leads the people of God to submit to the Word of God. You should see people seeking God's Word together, devoting themselves

to teaching and learning God's Word, and then discovering ways to apply God's Word to their lives.

*A Loving Church*
We live in a time where our society is becoming more
and more disjointed and divided. Families are falling
apart like never before. People are looking for a place
to "belong," a community where they can feel safe, a
family that will offer support and love. That is exactly
what the church should be. The believers in that first
church "devoted themselves to . . . fellowship." Fellowship refers to people caring for and looking out for
one another.

Now realize that no church is going to be perfect.
In fact, Satan hates the church and he does all that he
can to cause problems—from personality conflicts, to
disagreements, to outright divisions. You may be surprised to discover as you get involved in a church that
your church will have its share of problems. So don't
go out looking for a perfect church; look instead for a
mature church, a church that can handle the differ-
ences and difficulties in a mature and loving manner.

The Bible goes on to describe the kind of "fellowship" these early believers had: "All the believers were
together and had everything in common. Selling their
possessions and goods, they gave to anyone as he had
need. Every day they continued to meet together in
the temple courts. They broke bread in their homes
and ate together with glad and sincere hearts" (Acts

2:44-46, NIV). The Greek word that is used here is *koinonia*.

This is a difficult word to translate as it has so many shades of meaning including fellowship, communion, contribution, distribution, partnership and partaking to name a few. The communal situation that was initially established was especially workable for that time and place. The church was under intense persecution and many believers lost employment and housing, so there was this *koinonia* to draw upon.

The church did not continue in this communal pattern. The primary principle we can glean from their example is that these first-century Christians looked out for each other, and we should do the same in the twenty-first century.

The Bible compares people's involvement in a church to being in a family. It also compares it to being a part of a body. When one part of your body hurts, it all hurts. You know how it feels when you stub your toe or hit your thumb with a hammer. The body of Christ is like that. The Bible says, "The human body has many parts, but the many parts make up only one body. So it is with the body of Christ. . . . If one part suffers, all the parts suffer with it, and if one part is honored, all the parts are glad" (1 Corinthians 12:12, 26).

A healthy church overflows with love. The members are in a family that cares deeply about each individual. Right after writing about how the church is a body, Paul wrote an entire chapter about the importance of love. In 1 Corinthians 13:4-7 we read:

> Love is patient and kind. Love is not jealous or boastful or proud or rude. Love does not demand its own way. Love is not irritable, and it keeps no record of when it has been wronged. It is never glad about injustice but rejoices whenever the truth wins out. Love never gives up, never loses faith, is always hopeful, and endures through every circumstance.

This is the most comprehensive description of love in all of Scripture. Paul shines love through a prism and we see fifteen of its colors and hues. Each ray gives a different facet of love. These descriptions do not focus so much on what love is as on what love *does* and *does not.* The love Paul describes is active, not abstract or passive. It may not *feel* patient, but it *is* patient, it practices patience. It does not simply have kind feelings, it *is* kind and acts out that kindness.

Love is only fully love when it acts. John wrote, "Dear children, let us stop just saying we love each other; let us really show it by our actions" (1 John 3:18). A church should show this kind of love. You as a member will want to learn more and more about putting this kind of love into your life.

Look for a church that seems to be overflowing with love—love for God, each other, and lost people.

That is the kind of church that reflects the heart of Jesus Christ.

### A Worshiping Church

In that first church, the believers were also dedicated to "sharing in the Lord's Supper and in prayer." In other words, these people not only listened to sermons and fellowshiped, they also worshiped.

Let's define our terms here—what is worship anyway? Well, it goes back to how God created us. The Bible tells us that God has "planted eternity in the human heart" (Ecclesiastes 3:11). In other words, humans have a sense of eternity, a sense of someone greater than themselves, a sense of there being more to life. All people worship because worship is the fundamental difference between humans and animals. Animals do not worship. They have no sense of eternity. My dog doesn't sit in the backyard meditating on the love and holiness of God. In contrast, humans have eternity in their hearts, and this causes them to worship. If they are not worshiping the true God, they are worshiping something—some worship sports heroes, actors, musicians, some worship possessions, some worship themselves and their own pursuit of power and pleasure.

The word "worship" comes from the old English "worth-ship," which means to ascribe worth or value to something or someone. We should worship that which is worthy. A god of our own making is not worthy of worship.

I remember reading the story of Hideyoshi, a Japanese warlord who ruled over Japan in the late 1500s. He commissioned a colossal statue of Buddha for a shrine in Kyoto. It took fifty thousand men five years to build. The work had scarcely been completed when the earthquake of 1596 brought the roof of the shrine crashing down, wrecking the statue. In a rage, Hideyoshi shot an arrow at the fallen colossus, angry that he had worked so hard and the god could not even protect himself or his temple.

So it is with the gods we create for ourselves. Not so with God.

The Bible tells us about a choir in heaven joyfully singing of the "worth-ship" of Christ: "And they sang in a mighty chorus: 'The Lamb is worthy—the Lamb who was killed. He is worthy to receive power and riches and wisdom and strength and honor and glory and blessing'" (Revelation 5:12).

Jesus gave a great overview of the purpose of worship in his conversation with a woman at the well, recorded in John 4. At that time, the woman was lonely and miserable. She was thirsting for more than the water at the bottom of the well. In the course of their discussion, the woman turned the topic to places of worship. Jesus set the record straight, saying, "But the time is coming and is already here when true worshipers will worship the Father in spirit and in truth. The Father is looking for anyone who will worship him that way" (John 4:23). With these words, Jesus indicated the fundamental elements of true worship—worshiping "in spirit and in truth."

### In Truth

Let's start with the second one—"in truth." This refers to our view of God. The God we worship must be the true God. He must be the God who actually exists, the true and living God. We cannot worship our sentimental concept of God or our modern updated "made-over" version of God. You can't say, "I don't believe in a God who will judge people. The God I worship is loving and kind."

That is not the true God; therefore, that is not true worship.

The true God we worship is *truth*. This means that he is the true God, His knowledge and words are true, and he is the final standard of truth. The true God we worship is *holy;* in other words, his character is perfect in every way. The true God we worship is *righteous.* As holiness describes his character, righteousness describes how his holiness impacts his dealings with mankind.

But wait, there's more! The true God we worship is also *good.* The word *good* could be understood to mean that God is the final standard of good, and that all that God is and does is worthy of approval. The true God we worship is also *loving.* God's holiness makes him unapproachable by sinful humans; God's love meant that he could approach us. The true God we worship is *just*. This characteristic is closely related to his holiness and righteousness. Because of his justice, we read stories of his wrath against sin and evil in the pages of Scripture. Because of his justice, evil will eventually be judged.

This is the true God we worship. People cannot remake him in their own image and decide which attributes they like the most, dumping the attributes that make them uncomfortable. This is a package deal—all or nothing. Our worship is a response to our understanding of the greatness and "worth-ship" of our God.

### In Spirit

Your worship of God should be based in truth, but you must also worship God "in spirit" because worship engages the affections, the heart, and yes, the emotions. This doesn't mean that worship always has to be an emotional experience, but it will engage your emotions. And it should. Some people can be so focused on their emotions and "feelings" that they attempt to worship a God of their own making. At the same time, however, people can be so focused on theology that they do not express themselves to God with their spirits.

Warren Wiersbe writes:

The important thing is that we keep the right balance. There is today such an emphasis on Bible knowledge that we are in danger of ignoring, or even opposing, personal experience. While we must not base our theology on experience, neither must we debase our theology by divorcing it from experience. If true worship is the response of the whole person to God, then we dare not neglect the emotions.

People express their emotions at weddings, funerals, even football games! We're all made a bit differently. In a worship service, you might see someone who has his eyes tightly closed, his hands lifted high, singing loudly. You may see another with her head bowed, hands not lifted, singing softly. In reality, they both may be worshiping in spirit and in truth—just in different ways.

Some churches have less formal services. They want to encourage the raising of hands, clapping, and joyful singing. Other churches are much more formal, where worship is more quiet and serene. As long as God is the center, as long as he is being worshiped in spirit and in truth, as long as he is the focus, you have found a worshiping church.

Look for a worshiping church, a church that lifts up God and brings glory to his name.

### An Evangelistic Church

Finally, look for a church that is evangelistic. That's a big word meaning a church that is reaching out to nonbelievers and drawing them in, a church that is growing. Regarding that first church, the Bible says that "each day the Lord added to their group those who were being saved" (Acts 2:47). This church was growing by quantum leaps!

This doesn't mean that you need to seek out the largest church around, for it may not have some of the characteristics mentioned above. You don't need to find the most well-known church with the most famous pastor or the church with the most social outreach—again, it may be lacking in other foundational attributes.

One thing that is abundantly clear is that the first-century church dramatically impacted its world. It was a church on the move—a church that touched those around it. It was said of those believers (not as a compliment) that they "turned the world upside down" (Acts 17:6, KJV).

A truly evangelistic church has a burden for people who are not believers. It is not a church comfortable in its soft pews and pretty colors. It may indeed have those things, but it is always burdened for the lost of the world. Such a church has outreach programs that focus on bringing people to hear the gospel. It is a church filled not with spectators and observers, but with workers. The observers are many, the critics are many, but, as Jesus said, "the workers are few" (Matthew 9:37, NIV).

I believe if these other biblical principles are in play (worshiping, learning, and loving) the natural result will be evangelism. Healthy believers reproduce themselves. And that is important because it is a fact that new believers are the very lifeblood of the church. They bring a much-needed excitement and zeal into our ranks, while those who are more mature in the faith can take them under their wings and help them to grow spiritually.

Some might say that their church is not called to evangelism, but rather to worship or teaching, etc. But the truth is that *every* church is called to worship, teaching, and yes, evangelism.

In fact, you show me a church that is not having new believers join it and I will show you a church that is either headed toward or is already beginning to experience spiritual stagnation.

The church has a choice—evangelize or fossilize!

May God help you to find a strong, vibrant church where you can discover your spiritual gifts, where you can be blessed and be a blessing to others.

# Part Three

## JESUS IS MY LORD

*Therefore, since we have been made right in God's sight by faith, we have peace with God because of what Jesus Christ our Lord has done for us.*

—ROMANS 5:1

## OVERCOMING TEMPTATION

There is nothing quite like being transformed by the power of God. That transformation happens when you put your faith in Jesus Christ as your Lord and Savior. Suddenly, your life begins to change. Things you used to take great pleasure in now are seen for what they are—destructive, deadening, and empty. On the other hand, things you had no interest in before now suddenly come alive—like reading the Bible, praying, and worshiping with God's people.

You are personally discovering the truth of that verse that says, "Those who become Christians become new persons. They are not the same anymore, for the old life is gone. A new life has begun!" (2 Corinthians 5:17). You might even be saying to yourself, "I will never do those things I used to do in the 'old life' before I knew Christ!"

I don't want to burst your bubble, but I need to give you a reality check. Yes, it is true that you are indeed a "new person" just as that passage says. Yes, it is true that you have a new spiritual nature and power to do what God wants you to do. But it is equally true that you still have the potential to sin and do the wrong thing. The fact is, as a follower of Jesus Christ, you are going to be tempted to do wrong things. That doesn't mean you have to give in to the temptation; it simply means that the potential to fall—and fall big—is there. You need to be aware of that.

Now don't feel bad about this. The most godly people get tempted. Jesus himself was tempted by Satan in the wilderness. In fact, in the case of our Lord's temptation, it came directly after the Holy Spirit came upon him in the form of a dove. After the dove came the devil. After the blessing came the temptation. And the same will happen to you.

You might be doing the best you have ever done spiritually when suddenly, out of left field, comes a wicked temptation to do the wrong thing. There it is, creeping out from the shadows. Something that has always been a problem for you—a bad habit, an unhealthy desire, a sinful act. You want to give in—even just once. Perhaps you do. That string of swear words; that seductive magazine; that forbidden internet site; that piece of juicy gossip; that "little" lie.

You feel a strong pull—it's amazing how strong! What is this about? Is it all over? Maybe you never became a Christian at all! No, it isn't over; and yes, you are still a Christian. You have simply faced that most universal of Satan's ammunition: Temptation.

Temptation is a reality of the Christian life. We

would prefer not to be tempted at all, for then we would not be so vulnerable to failure. Yet it may surprise you to know that temptation can have a positive effect! It's been said, "Christians are a lot like teabags. You don't know what they're made of until you put them in hot water."

Everyone faces temptation in one way, shape, or form on a daily basis. When James was writing about temptation, he began, "When tempted, no one should say . . ." (James 1:13, NIV). Notice that he didn't say "*If* you are tempted," but "*when*." In other words, temptation is inevitable. No one escapes it. Not even ministers. I heard the story of a minister who parked his car in a "No Parking" zone in a large city. He was short of time and couldn't find a single space. So under his windshield wiper, he placed a note written on his business card. It read, "I have circled the block 10 times. I have an appointment to keep. 'Forgive us our trespasses.'" When he returned, he found a ticket from a police officer along with this note, "Dear Reverend, I've circled this block for 10 years. If I don't give you a ticket, I lose my job. 'Lead us not into temptation.'"

## The Source

You might ask, "Where does temptation come from? Who's responsible?" There are a couple of answers, for temptation comes from outside as well as from within. We have both external foes and internal foes.

You see, when you became a Christian, you joined the enemy army. Satan, who had you on his side before, is angry that you have defected. Needless to say, he did not want you coming to Christ in the first place, and did everything in his power to keep you from it. But having failed in that, he has another strategy that, though not as desirable as keeping a person from faith, is almost as effective. The devil wants to immobilize you. He wants to make you ineffective in this new Christian life, paralyzed by guilt or shame. The way he will begin this attack is through temptation. He has been sizing you up for some time now, and he will hit you where you are potentially weak and vulnerable. You will find that temptations are very personal. He will not necessarily tempt me in the same way he tempts you because I have weaknesses in different areas than you do.

Temptations are often also perfectly timed. When you are at your weakest (discouraged, tired, frustrated, sad), that's when Satan strikes you with the temptation to which you may be most vulnerable. History tells us that when Hitler invaded Europe during the early years of World War II, in almost every situation he attacked on a weekend. Hitler knew that the various governments would not be in session, making it more difficult to react swiftly to an invasion. In the same way, our enemy, the devil, also waits for an opportune time to attack. He may wait until you feel weak. Yet other times, he may send a temptation after a time of great spiritual growth, success, or even blessing. He knows then that you may be off guard, that you may feel invincible. In any case, be ready, because temptation *will* strike you. Forewarned is forearmed.

Some people think that just as there is an all-powerful God in heaven, so there is an equally powerful devil in hell. But that is wrong. Consider these contrasts:

- God is omniscient (all knowing), but Satan's knowledge, though vast, is clearly limited.
- God is omnipotent (all powerful), but Satan, though a mighty enemy, has clear limitations to what he can do.
- God is omnipresent (present everywhere at all times), but Satan can only be in one place at one time.

Most people do not face temptation directly from Satan himself, but from one of his many minions instead. The demonic powers are well organized and act upon the devil's bidding.

The apostle Paul, speaking of these demonic forces, wrote, "For we are not fighting against people made of flesh and blood, but against the evil rulers and authorities of the unseen world, against those mighty powers of darkness who rule this world, and against wicked spirits in the heavenly realms" (Ephesians 6:12).

Satan works with two close allies: the world and the flesh. What exactly is "the world" to which the Bible refers? First of all, it is not referring to the earth itself. In other words, when you admire a beautiful sunset or any of the other myriad things that God created, that is not a "worldly" act. Indeed, Scripture tells us, "The earth is the LORD's, and all its fullness, the world and those who dwell therein" (Psalm 24:1, NKJV). Sometimes, the word "world" refers to something altogether different from the earth. It is speaking of a system, a way of thinking, that is hostile to God. It's the basic, selfish "me first" attitude of so many today, the attitude of people who live primarily for personal gratification without a thought given to their souls or the God who created them.

John gives one of the most concise definitions of the "world": "For all that is in the world—the lust of the flesh, the lust of the eyes, and the pride of life—is not of the Father but is of the world" (1 John 2:16, NKJV). This is not new; the world has been that way for a long time: "We know that we are children of God and that the world around us is under the power and control of the evil one" (1 John 5:19). The devil is referred to as "the god of this evil world" (2 Corinthians 4:4). Satan and the "world" are your external enemies, seeking to tempt you to do evil. The "flesh" and your personal desires are your internal enemies, as you discover in the next section.

## The Seduction

James wrote, "Temptation comes from the lure of our own evil desires. These evil desires lead to evil actions, and evil actions lead to death" (James 1:14-15). Satan may be the author, but without question, people play a part in their own temptations. Satan needs your cooperation in this area; if there is no desire on your part, then there is no temptation. And when you give in, you cannot blame Satan or your circumstances; instead, you must take responsibility for your own actions.

That's easier said than done in this culture of "victims." Everyone seems to have an excuse for everything. That strategy was tried by the first couple. When caught in his sin, Adam did not accept responsibility, but instead blamed God for giving him the woman who had tempted him! Eve, in turn, blamed the serpent. Read the story in Genesis 3. So today everyone tries to say that they had no choice, they were forced, it's in their genes so they can't help it, or even that the devil made them do it. They couldn't be more wrong.

In most cases, temptation enters through the doorway of your mind. When Satan wanted to lead the first man and woman into sin, he started by attacking the woman's mind. The apostle Paul wrote, regarding temptation, "I am afraid that just as Eve was deceived by the serpent's cunning, your minds may somehow be led astray" (2 Corinthians 11:3, NIV). Why the mind? Because it is there that people reason, contemplate, and fantasize. Your mind can reach into the past through memories and into the future through imagination. Satan gets you to "just think about it," whatever "it" (the temptation) may be for you.

For Satan to succeed, you must listen to him and, most importantly, you must desire what he offers. Again, "Temptation comes from the lure of our own evil desires" (James 1:14). The word *lure* suggests a juicy worm being dangled in front of a fish. The fish's desire causes it to bite, and with that bite, the fish gets more than it bargained for! Satan will use different types of bait to tempt you as well.

And that's the tricky thing about temptation: It is so—well—tempting! Satan is not a fool. His poison is generally candy-coated. When Eve was tempted by the fruit in the Garden of Eden, Satan told her that eating the mysterious fruit would open her eyes and make her wise. Eve then rationalized that the fruit "looked so fresh and delicious" (Genesis 3:6). The fruit Eve ate is often described as an apple, though the Bible says no such thing. Who knows? It may have been a fruit such as has never been seen and will never be seen again! It may have even pulsated! Whatever the case, something has to be alluring, otherwise it will not be tempting. But it is important to note that it is the bite, not the bait, that constitutes the temptation. Had Eve resisted, it all would have been fine. But she didn't, and the rest, as they say, is history.

A temptation is going to be appealing. And if you work hard enough, you can rationalize anything. Never mind the consequences or long-term effects, this is something you want *right now.* You may say, "I'll know when to stop," or "Everyone's doing it," or "I'm not hurting anybody." Make no mistake—you start to rationalize and you will soon be in sin. That's why temptation works so well—for Satan.

At times, you will fall. Hopefully at many more times, you will overcome. When you fall, you can get up, ask God for forgiveness, and learn your lesson. Try to "fail forward," which simply means "learn from your mistakes." When you are victorious, don't shine your medals just yet. For in pride you can be even more vulnerable. Instead, you must learn methods for overcoming temptation and be ready to face it every day.

## The Solution

Temptation is difficult; the seduction can, at times, seem to be too much to bear. In order to get a handle on what you're facing and to know how to deal with it, you need to understand a few things.

### Everyone Faces Temptation

The word "tempt" means "to entice to wrong by a promise of pleasure or gain." All believers experience temptation, yet it is clear that Satan focuses his attacks on those who are young in the faith and those who are making a difference in God's kingdom. Immediately after you accepted Christ, you may have been plagued with doubts about whether God had truly forgiven you. Those were from Satan, who set his sights on you and hoped to bring you down in flames before you could do any more damage to him and his kingdom.

You have probably had thoughts like, "What if Christ really did not come into my life?" or "Maybe I just psyched myself into this," or "What if this is not true and I believe a lie?" Do you think those thoughts are unique to you? The Bible says, "Remember that the temptations that come into your life are no different from what others experience" (1 Corinthians 10:13). In other words, we all face what you may think is unique to you. Satan uses the same tactics generation after generation with great effect. The attack of challenging the validity of your conversion or the fact that God has indeed spoken to you goes all the way back to the Garden of Eden. Take heart. The very fact that you are being attacked in this area shows you are on the right course!

I can remember the first time I encountered serious temptation as a brand-new Christian. I had just made a commitment to follow Jesus, and I was told by other more seasoned believers to beware of temptation. I wasn't quite sure what they were talking about because, at that point, I suppose I subscribed to Oscar Wilde's statement about eliminating temptation when he said,

"The only way I know of getting rid of temptation is by giving in to it." Prior to my conversion, I pretty much did what I wanted when I wanted. So here I was, a brand new follower of Jesus trying to figure out when my first actual temptation would come knocking.

When it came, there was no denying its presence.

There was a very attractive girl in one of my high school classes that I secretly had a crush on, but who never paid any attention to me— that is, until I received Christ.

One Friday, out of the blue, she came up to me, introduced herself, and then said she found me very attractive. I wondered why this same girl who didn't even seem to know I existed just days before would suddenly say that. I thought, *Is this the temptation the Christians were warning me about?* What she said next confirmed to me that, indeed, it was.

With a "come hither" look, she told me her parents were out of town for the weekend and she was wondering if I would like to spend the weekend with her, just the two of us!

Then I knew I was being tempted! Why? Because quite frankly, things like that just didn't happen to me. I was actually kind of thrilled—not by the offer from the girl, for it was far too ridiculous and obvious to even take seriously. Rather, I was thrilled by the confirmation that I was on the right track following Jesus. So much so, in fact, that Satan was already trying to pull me down!

## *It Is Not a Sin to Be Tempted*

Even Jesus faced temptation. He was sinless, so obviously being tempted is not a sin. It is giving in to temptation and sinning that is, well, sin. Jesus felt the presence and pressure of temptation just like you do. He understands how it is for you when you are tempted, and he knows how to help you. Hebrews 2:18 says, "Since he himself has gone through suffering and temptation, he is able to help us when we are being tempted."

## *Being "Tested" Is Different from Being "Tempted"*

There is a difference between being "tested" and being "tempted." God may test his followers to teach them lessons and to bring out the good in them. For example, you may face difficulty in your life, a trial that God has allowed in order to "test" your faith and help it to grow. James wrote about this too: "Dear brothers and sisters, whenever trouble comes your way, let it be an opportunity for joy. For when your faith is tested, your endurance has a chance to grow" (James 1:2-3).

Every difficulty you face is an opportunity to trust in God. Sometimes, however, you may face a difficulty and be angry at God or feel that he has abandoned you. You are being tempted to turn away from God so that you won't trust in him and won't learn what he wants you to learn. That comes from Satan. He tempts you in order to bring you down. Jesus de-

scribed Satan as being like a "thief" who only desires
to "steal and kill and destroy" (John 10:10).

### Don't Under- or Overestimate
### Temptation's Seduction

Some believers feel that they are helpless against
temptation. For many people, however, resisting
temptation is difficult only because they truly don't
want to discourage temptation completely. They pray
to be delivered from temptation but would like to
keep in touch. But remember this: to pray against
temptation and yet to rush into places where you are
most vulnerable is like thrusting your fingers into the
fire and then praying that you won't get burned. To
underestimate temptation's power is a big mistake.

A number of years ago, I was out swimming with
my youngest son, Jonathan, who was then around
five years old. I took him out where the waves were
breaking and suddenly found myself being pulled by
a rather powerful riptide. When this happens, you're
supposed to swim parallel with the shore until you
get out of it, but this riptide seemed to have a mind
all its own, pulling me and Jonathan along quite
swiftly. The irony was that I was not very far at all
from the shore, so I was sure once I got my feet back
on the sand in the water I would be able to walk back
to shore. But it wasn't that easy—I simply could not
plant my feet. Finally a lifeguard came toward us with
a flotation device. I actually waved him away—saying

we were fine. But we weren't fine and, fortunately, he ignored me. Just as he got to me, I was able to plant my feet on the sand and walk out. We were safe, but that riptide had certainly tried to take me and Jonathan places that we didn't want to go!

Temptation can seem that way too. We sometimes laugh at it, thinking we can easily handle it. The next thing we know, we're being pulled out to sea. Do not underestimate the power of temptation.

The evangelist Billy Sunday once said, "One reason that sin flourishes is that it is treated like a cream puff instead of a rattlesnake." The author of temptation is Satan, and you need to have a healthy respect for your enemy, just as you need to have a healthy respect for the ocean.

At the same time, however, don't overestimate Satan's abilities and powers. As already noted, Satan would like you to think that he is equal with God, but that is not true. Satan has limited powers. He had to get permission to cause Job's suffering (Job 1:9-12). The demons could not enter the herd of pigs without Jesus' permission (Matthew 8:31-32). God puts a hedge around his people, and Satan cannot go beyond what God allows.

Not only has God set a hedge of protection around you, but he will never let you face more than you can handle. This promise is recorded in 1 Corinthians 10:13: "But remember that the temptations that come into your life are no different from what others expe-

rience. And God is faithful. He will keep the temptation from becoming so strong that you can't stand up
against it. When you are tempted, he will show you a
way out so that you will not give in to it."

### Know That God Will Help You

Temptation comes, but you can overcome and be
stronger spiritually as a result. How do you overcome? By knowing that God will help you when you
are tempted. Stay close to God who promises to be
faithful to you. Remember that the Holy Spirit lives
within you, and "the Spirit who lives in you is greater
than the spirit who lives in the world" (1 John 4:4).

The Bible describes a time when Jesus was "led out
into the wilderness by the Holy Spirit to be tempted
there by the devil" (Matthew 4:1). He was within the
will of God, needing to face this temptation. Notice
that it was *after* forty days of fasting that the devil
came. He waited until Jesus was famished and then
came to offer—guess what?—*bread*. Not only that,
Satan deftly couched his temptations in Scripture.
Jesus had every rationale laid out on the table for
him. Except that Jesus knew better. He knew the enemy—and so must you. And you must know your
Bible, so you are ready to fight back, as Jesus did.

Jesus used the Bible back at Satan—except Jesus
used it correctly, of course. Jesus knew the book and,
in doing so, gave a model of how to win over temptation. All believers must read and become familiar

with God's Word in order to keep from becoming casualties in these ongoing spiritual battles. The success or failure of your Christian life depends on how much of the Bible you get into your heart and mind on a regular basis—and how obedient you are to what you read! If you neglect to study Scripture, your spiritual life will completely unravel.

You must make it a top priority to read, study, and memorize the Word of God. It's a good idea to carry a Bible in your briefcase, pocket, or purse—but the best place to carry it is in your heart. Once Scripture is ingrained in your memory, it will always be there to use when those temptations strike. A psalm writer said it this way, "I have hidden your word in my heart, that I might not sin against you" (Psalm 119:11). Your mind must be so saturated with God's Word that it will be like a "spiritual computer" so that when you face decisions or temptations, you automatically remember the Scriptures that relate to that particular situation.

It might impress you to know that it is the ministry of the Holy Spirit to bring God's Word to your mind when you need it: "But when the Father sends the Counselor as my representative—and by the Counselor I mean the Holy Spirit—he will teach you everything and will remind you of everything I myself have told you" (John 14:26). But the Holy Spirit cannot "remind" you of something you have not learned!

This is an important foundational truth to remember in temptation. You do not fight *for* victory—you fight *from* it. In other words, the war has already been won; Satan is a defeated enemy. So you are battling from the winning side. What a great blessing it is when you have stood up to temptation and been victorious!

Yes, temptation is all around you. Remember, God is not responsible for your temptation. He allows it, but he always puts a hedge of protection around you. Temptation can be endured and overcome because God will be with you through it. When you overcome temptation, you will be stronger spiritually.

And that's a great victory! So onward, Christian soldier!

# 7

## DEALING WITH PROBLEMS

Have you noticed how very few people take responsibility for anything anymore? Most people don't want to take responsibility for their own actions. There is always someone else to blame for the problems.

If there's trouble at home, the problem is the kids or the spouse or the parents.

If there's trouble at work, the problem is the boss or the coworkers.

If there's trouble with life in general, the problem is the dysfunctional family the person grew up in.

There are a million and one excuses that people use to pardon their wrong behavior.

"I wouldn't have done it if you hadn't done what you did!"

"I do those things because that's the way my father (or mother) always acted."

"Maybe I shouldn't have done it, but you're just as bad!"

What these people are really saying is, "I am not personally responsible for my own actions. Everything I do is someone else's fault."

Pathetic, isn't it?

In his book *A Nation of Victims*, Charles Sikes writes, "The politics of victimization have taken the place of more traditional expressions of morality and equity. If you lose a job, you can sue over the mental distress of being fired. If your bank goes broke, the government will insure your deposit. If you drive drunk and crash, you can sue someone for failing to warn you" (quoted in *The Vanishing Conscience* by John MacArthur). Our problems, we are told, are the result of being "victims." There is always someone else to blame, someone who hurt us. No one is guilty anymore.

Nowadays, people are placing psychology on the same level (and sometimes above) the Bible. Many in the church today know more about "self-esteem" than about self-denial. They know more about "inner healing" than about outward obedience. They know more about how to "get in touch with the inner child" than about how to "reckon the old self to be dead."

Okay, so what really is the source of our problems? Is it low self-esteem? Is it the fault of others? Is it our family, race, or culture? None of the above. And wouldn't you know it—the Bible happens to give us the answer to the source of our problems. (That should come as no surprise by now—the Bible has answers to everything!)

## Look Within

James asks the question, "What is causing the quarrels and fights among you? Isn't it the whole army of evil desires at war within you?" (James 4:1). In other words, what's causing all the problems? You are! You are causing all kinds of problems because the evil desires within you are the problem. Now don't try separating out those desires and blaming them and not you. You can try—but it won't work!

The Greek word for "desires" is *hedone,* from which we derive our word *hedonism*—the belief that pleasure is the chief good in life. If hedonism had a "patron saint," it would surely be Hugh Hefner, a man who has abandoned himself to the pursuit of pleasure. But the problem is, when all you seek is your own pleasure, when that is your god, then the obvious result is going to be conflict and the myriad problems that go along with it.

It is important to note that pleasure itself is not necessarily sinful or wrong. The Bible says in Psalm 16:11, "You will show me the way of life, granting me the joy of your presence and the *pleasures* of living with you forever" (italics mine). The Bible often speaks of the joy of the Lord and the true happiness that comes from God. Also consider Psalm 84:11, "No good thing will the LORD withhold from those who do what is right." Or 1 Timothy 6:17, "Trust . . . in the living God, who gives us richly all things to enjoy" (NKJV). Clearly, our lives are meant to be lived with joy and enjoyment of all that God has provided for us.

However, when people have personal pleasure as the driving force of their lives, they will find soon find themselves "running on empty." In the parable of the sower, Jesus described people who "hear and accept the [gospel] message, but all too quickly the message is crowded out by the cares and riches and *pleasures* of this life. And so they never grow into maturity" (Luke 8:14, italics mine). Titus 3:3 refers to those who are "slaves to many wicked desires and evil pleasures." Peter speaks of false teachers who "love to indulge in evil pleasures" and are a "disgrace" (2 Peter 2:13). People who focus on evil pleasures, who make pleasure the god of their lives, will never be content, never really happy, and constantly in conflict. Think about it—if a person is constantly seeking only pleasure, how will that person be as a spouse, an employee, a parent, a friend, a coworker?

You see, the pursuit of pleasure rarely brings what one is searching for, but rather, emptiness. Someone has said, "The best cure for hedonism is an attempt to practice it." One only has to read the writings of Solomon in Ecclesiastes to see this. Look at Ecclesiastes 2:1-2, "I said to myself, 'Come now, let's give pleasure a try. Let's look for the "good things" in life.' But I found that this, too, was meaningless. It is silly to be laughing all the time,' I said. 'What good does it do to seek only pleasure?'" The intense desire to please ourselves is, in many cases, the ultimate source of our problems. Joy Davidman (wife of C. S. Lewis) made this insightful statement about the pursuit of pleasure: "Living for his own pleasure is the least pleasurable thing a man can do; if his neighbors don't kill him in disgust, he will die slowly of boredom and powerlessness" (from *Smoke on the Mountain*).

What's so bad about taking care of ourselves? As pleasure can be either good or evil, so can that desire to care for oneself. We hear so much in the church today about self-esteem, self-worth, self-image. Some even try to say that "sin is the loss of self-esteem." I disagree, and more importantly, so does the Bible. Do you think that God wants us to feel good about ourselves—have high self-esteem—while we are living in sin? Listen to these verses: "Wash your hands, you sinners; purify your hearts, you hypocrites. Let there be tears for the wrong things you have done. Let there be sorrow and deep grief. Let there be sadness instead of laughter, and gloom instead of joy" (James 4:8-9). Does that sound like God is calling you to high self-esteem?

Consider how the apostle Paul felt when he faced his own sinfulness. "Oh, what a miserable person I am!" (Romans 7:24). At that point, Paul did not have very high self-esteem.

Consider Jesus' parable about the Pharisee and the tax collector. "Then Jesus told this story to some who had great self-confidence and scorned everyone else" (Luke 18:9). The proud Pharisee thanked God that he was not a sinner like everyone else, and especially that he was not as bad as the tax collector. The tax collector, on the other hand, with very little self-esteem, cried out to God for mercy and forgiveness. Jesus said, "This sinner, not the Pharisee, returned home justified before God. For the proud will be humbled, but the humble will be honored" (Luke 18:14).

Because "self" is the problem that causes our problems, how do we deal with it? Well, the Bible tells us that, too. Jesus said, "If any of you wants to be my follower, you must put aside your selfish ambition, shoulder your cross daily, and follow me" (Luke 9:23).

I can hear you saying, "Now wait a minute, Greg! I didn't bank on all this. I'm just now getting my life together, and you're telling me chuck it all, have no fun, and have low self-esteem?"

No, I'm certainly not saying that. If you have come to Christ as your Savior, you are indeed getting a handle on life, real life. And I already told you that you can still have lots of pleasure in this life, in the right way, for God has granted that to you as a gift from him. And being a Christian actually gives you the best self-esteem possible. For only believers truly understand where they came from, who they are, and why they are here. You were created by a loving God, you have purpose, and you will find your life's work as you follow Christ.

Let me give you a couple of verses to calm your fears.

O LORD, you have examined my heart and know everything about me. . . . You chart the

path ahead of me and tell me where to stop and
rest. Every moment you know where I am. . . .
You both precede and follow me. You place
your hand of blessing on my head. . . . You
made all the delicate, inner parts of my body
and knit me together in my mother's womb. . .
. You saw me before I was born. Every day of
my life was recorded in your book. . . . How
precious are your thoughts about me, O God!
They are innumerable! I can't even count them;
they outnumber the grains of sand! And when
I wake up in the morning, you are still with me!
(from Psalm 139)

There, do you feel better? There is no better self-
esteem than the esteem that comes from God. He
knew you before you were born. He knit you together
in your mother's womb. He is with you every moment. He has a plan for your life.

Yet even as a believer, you will struggle with what
is called your "old nature." You have become a Christian, and God has cleansed you from all sin. He sees
you as righteous and holy because of the shed blood
of his Son. Yet while you are on this earth in this human body, you will still sin. You will still mess up,
make mistakes, and deal with that "old nature" or
"old self" that tries to rear its ugly head. So you'll create some problems for yourself.

The old nature could be compared to a weed, and

the new nature to a beautiful flower. Let's say you just purchased a new bulb and carefully planted it into fertile soil. You watered it daily and kept all dangers like hungry snails at bay. You were thrilled when your little bulb took root and broke ground. At the same time, however, a weed broke through a crack in the sidewalk, and without any nurture or care, grew into an eight-foot tree!

The same can be true of your old and new natures. Much like that tender flower, we need to nurture ourselves spiritually through prayer, Bible study, fellowship, obedience to God and more. But the old nature doesn't need much encouragement to flourish. It's like that weed. It will pretty much grow anywhere, anytime. If you fail to build up the new nature, it's only a matter of time until that old nature will be in control again.

I heard the story of a man from India who compared his old and new natures to two dogs who were constantly fighting with each other. When asked what dog would win, his reply was "The one I feed the most, of course!"

The same is true of our new and old natures. The one we "feed the most" is the one that will win. By reading this book, you have made a conscious choice to "feed the right dog!"

You'll also face problems that are no fault of your own. You are still in a world filled with many unsaved people who will do their best to create problems for you. (I'm sure you could name a few.) So you have to learn a new way of responding to all of these problematic people. And problems also come from living in a world where things just can be difficult—storms can damage your home, your car needs repairs, bills need to be paid, jobs need to be gotten (or left).

In any case, becoming a Christian doesn't leave all your problems behind. The problems you had yesterday before you became a believer may well still be your problems today. Of course, the biggest and most profound difference is you are now not alone in dealing with those problems. Jesus Christ himself has come and taken residence in your heart as your Savior and your Lord.

Not only that, he has also given you "The User's Manual of Life" to guide you—the Bible.

The question now becomes, "How do you, as a new believer, deal with these problems according to the Bible?"

## Same Problems, New Perspective

With God in your life, every problem that occurs is not to be blamed on somebody. Instead, it can be seen as an opportunity for you to exercise your newfound faith. In other words, the problem can defeat you or cause you to act in all kinds of ways that would not be pleasing to God (you know what I mean!). Or the problem can be seen as a chance to prove your faith in God. You can watch the Holy Spirit guide you through the situation, help you act correctly, even work a miracle sometimes! You can have a whole new perspective! In other words, you can do what James recommended to the believers to whom he wrote.

Just as a little background, the epistle of James was written by James, the half-brother of Jesus himself! It is interesting to note that James never utilized "executive privilege" by reminding the church he was the Lord's actual half-brother. Talk about name dropping!

But then there would have been the unique challenges of having Jesus Christ as your older brother. It is noteworthy that none of Jesus' brothers and sisters believed in him prior to his resurrection (John 7:5). This just goes to show that even a perfect and flawless life is not necessarily enough to convince someone of the truth of the gospel. So what changed James' mind? It was the resurrection of Jesus from the dead and a personal appearance our Lord made to him (1 Corinthians 15:7).

James became the leader of the church in Jerusalem. He wrote this letter to people who suffered. As Louis Evans points out in his commentary on James:

> The Epistle of James was written to people who suffered. It was written to demonstrate that Christianity, as James knew it, was a metal that can withstand the fires of adversity; it is a rock that withstands the erosion of storm and tempest and wear. Christianity is no greenhouse

faith. It is not an opiate for the beaten and fearful: it is a cure. It is not faith that only holds firm only when there are no pressures; rather it is a faith that holds us steady in spite of the trials that come like tempests against us.

James led the church in Jerusalem, made up mostly of converted Jews, but he wrote to Jewish believers scattered all over the world. Many believers had scattered because of the persecution they had faced in Jerusalem (see Acts 8:1). Yet going elsewhere did not make them immune to difficulty, trials, and even persecution. James knew that his flock needed encouragement, and so he wrote to them.

At the very beginning of this letter, he encourages, "Whenever trouble comes your way, let it be an opportunity for joy. For when your faith is tested, your endurance has a chance to grow" (James 1:2-3).

Whoa! Wait a minute. He just put "trouble" and "joy" in the same sentence. Weird? Not really. He's talking about attitude. How do you look at your troubles and problems? As things to excuse or blame on someone else, or as an opportunity for joy and spiritual growth? Just as a muscle does not grow without exercise, so your brand-new "spiritual muscles" are going to be soft and flabby if your life is too easy. God knows that. So the problems that come your way are part of your exercise routine to build up those muscles and help you "grow."

Realize this: When James talks about being joyful in the midst of trouble, he doesn't mean that you have to be happy that the trouble has come along. That would be unnatural. Nor is he saying that you should enjoy your trials. No one can do that. Trials, by their very nature, are not enjoyable. If they were, they wouldn't be trials!

Instead, James is saying that we need to make a deliberate and careful decision to experience joy in our troubles and trials. Do you think that is possible? Consider Paul and Silas. They experienced great trouble after arriving in Philippi with the gospel. They were flogged (meaning their backs were ripped open with whips) and they were thrown in prison and put in the stocks. The Bible records what happened next: "Around midnight, Paul and Silas were praying and singing hymns to God, and the other prisoners were listening" (Acts 16:25). Do you think they felt joyful? Probably not at first. But they knew that they were completely in God's hands, and so they left their problems with him and decided to be joyful.

So yes, it's possible.

But it's not necessarily easy.

## New Life, New Lessons

The first thing that usually comes to our minds when we face a time of difficulty is, "Why?" We ask, "God, why are you allowing this to happen to me? What have I done to deserve this?"

God often doesn't answer our "why" question. When Job asked it in the Old Testament after facing severe trials, God didn't explain why. We can take comfort in the fact that God allows difficulties into our lives because he has lessons he wants us to learn. A trial may be no more than a pop quiz to see if we've learned the material. Sooner or later we have to learn the material and pass the test before we can move forward.

I remember when I was in school my heart would always sink when the teacher would say "We're having a pop quiz today!" The reason for that, of course, is because I was rarely, if ever, prepared. There were always those students who took some perverse pleasure in "pop quizzes" and such. (We used to call them "nerds" and "geeks." Now we probably call them "Boss"!)

Anyway, God gives pop quizzes too. He rarely announces them ahead of time; they just come. It was like that in school; it's like that in the Christian life. God wants you to mature and grow; you can't do that unless you have a chance to flex your faith muscles in the face of difficulties.

Sometimes we think we know it all. Even new believers can sometimes get a little bit cocky. We think we have the answers and can tell everyone how to live. Then the Lord, through a test, says in essence, "All right. Let's see how well you've been listening." God doesn't do this to be cruel; quite the contrary. He wants us to be strong, mature believers.

Consider the way a mother eagle teaches her little eaglets to fly. When the time comes for the baby eaglet to try its wings (which the mother knows instinctively), the mother bird pushes her young out of the nest. She will let the frightened baby drop a distance of ninety feet or more before she swoops down under it and carries it back to safety. This is repeated about every fifteen minutes until the little eaglet begins to fly on its own. To an onlooker, this may seem cruel. Yet if the baby eagles are not shoved out, they would be content to remain in the nest forever.

Why does God shove us out of the nest? So we will learn how to fly! That's what problems, trials, troubles, difficulties—whatever name you give them—do for us. They teach us how to fly!

Jesus once gave a pop quiz to his disciples. The story is recorded in John 6. The multitudes were gathering, wanting to hear Jesus teach. Lunchtime came and everyone was getting hungry. "Jesus soon saw a great crowd of people climbing the hill, looking for him. Turning to Philip he asked, 'Philip, where can we buy bread to feed all these people?' He was testing Philip, for he already knew what he was going to do" (John 6:5-6). Philip looked at the obvious impossibility of the task and answered that it would take a small fortune to buy enough food to feed the crowd. Another disciple, Andrew, pointed out the small boy's lunch, but also commented that it was worthless with such a huge crowd.

Jesus wanted to see if his boys were learning anything. He asked Philip what he was going to do, and Philip answered that it was impossible. Andrew, in even mentioning the boy's small lunch, seemed to almost catch what Jesus was saying. If Philip got an F for failing, then Andrew got a C for effort.

The test was, "Do you believe God cares even about these people and their hunger?" And he asks you, when you face a difficulty, "Do you believe that God cares even about you and this situation?"

Have you ever faced a situation when you had no food to eat? Or money to pay your bills? I have. After walking with the Lord for over thirty years, I can say that he has always provided for my needs. And that's a promise for all of us from God's Word, "And this same God who takes care of me [Paul] will supply all your needs from his glorious riches, which have been given to us in Christ Jesus" (Philippians 4:19). Notice it says he will supply all our needs, not all our greeds.

It happens. These times of trouble are also God's way of testing you.

Will you pass or fail?

While I can't answer all of the "whys" for your particular situation, there are some general truths about problems that will be helpful to you.

*First, God's ultimate purpose for you is that you might be conformed into the image of his Son.* His usual method for this is "heavenly pressure" in order to produce a family likeness. Some trials will show immediate results in our lives; others are more "long term," such as dealing with irritating people, difficult circumstances, emotional lows, or even tragedy, such as the loss of a loved one. But even the long-term trials are temporary. "For our present troubles are quite small and won't last very long. Yet they produce for us an immeasurably great glory that will last forever!" (2 Corinthians 4:17).

I remember hearing Warren Wiersbe say that when God permits his children to go through the furnace, he keeps his eye on the clock and his hand on the thermostat. If we rebel, he may have to reset the clock. If we submit, he will not permit us to suffer one minute too long.

Are you in such a situation right now? Are you backed up against a wall with no way to look but up? Cheer up! God is still in the miracle business. God may be testing you right now. Let's work on getting a good grade! While this process may not be enjoyable, remember that God's ultimate aim is to make us like Jesus.

*Second, God allows trials so that you will become strong spiritually.* Trials and testings produce necessary qualities in our lives. Remember what James said, "When your faith is tested, your endurance has a chance to grow." Endurance is also translated patience, steadfastness, fortitude, perseverance. James is talking about "staying power" and "toughness." God wants iron to enter your soul. Why? "For when your endurance is fully developed, you will be strong in character and ready for anything" (James 1:4).

A traveler visiting a logging area in the Northwest United States watched with great curiosity as a lumberjack working alongside a mountain stream periodically jabbed his sharp hook into a log as it passed by to separate it from the others. The traveler asked the logger what he was doing.

The logger replied, "These logs may all look alike to you, but I can recognize that a few of them are quite different. The ones I let pass come from trees that grow in a valley where they were always protected from the storms. Their grain is rather coarse. The logs I have pulled aside come from high up on the mountains where they were beaten by strong winds from the time they were quite small. This toughens the trees and gives them a fine grain. We save these logs for choice work. They are too good to be used for ordinary lumber."

In the same way, God has selected you for a choice work. But before he can use you, he must toughen the grain of your life. He does this by allowing you to go through problems and difficulties so that your faith can be tested and purified, and so that you have "staying power." God wants to toughen you up and help you to mature spiritually.

*Third, God promises to be with you as you go though the problem.* God is with you and in control of even the most desperate of circumstances. The disciples saw this firsthand. They all got into a boat to cross the Sea of Galilee and Jesus, exhausted, fell asleep. A storm arose (as they often do on that large lake) and the disciples were soon in fear for their lives. But Jesus slept on. He needed physical sleep for his weary body. But the moment the disciples cried out to him, he awoke and answered their need—miraculously (Mark 4:35-41).

The Lord will do the same for you in the midst of your trials. Sometimes he just lets you reach the point of desperation so that you will recognize that he is your only hope. As a child of God, you have the promise that God's presence is with you in the midst of the storm. He will not leave you stranded in the middle of your problem. Although he doesn't promise smooth sailing, he does promise a safe passage.

In his famous psalm, David wrote, "Yea, though I walk through the valley of the shadow of death, I will fear no evil: for thou art with me; thy rod and thy staff they comfort me" (Psalm 23:4, KJV). Notice David did not say, "Though I collapse in the valley."

God will get you to the other side. He is with you as you walk through your "fiery trials" of life.

A powerful example of this is the story of those three Hebrew teenagers, Shadrach, Meshach, and Abednego. Because they would not bow before an idol, the king cast them into a fiery furnace. But the Bible tells us that they were not alone, for walking with them in the midst of this horrible trial was the Lord himself. Even the King recognized it, for upon peering into the flames, he saw Shadrach, Meshach, and Abednego strolling around in the furnace like it was a walk in the park. He said in astonishment, "Look! . . . I see four men loose, walking in the midst of the fire; and they are not hurt, and the form of the fourth is like the Son of God" (Daniel 3:25, NKJV)

In the same way, Jesus walks with you through your trials too. He said, "When you pass through the waters, I will be with you; and through the rivers, they shall not overflow you. When you walk through the fire, you shall not be burned, nor shall the flame scorch you" (Isaiah 43:2, NKJV).

*Fourth, God can give you peace and hope, even in the middle of the most difficult problems.* God knows when you are facing difficulty, and he knows how afraid, worried, or upset you are. No matter how difficult the trial, you know that you can trust in God. Jesus promised his disciples, "I am leaving you with a gift—peace of mind and heart. And the peace I give isn't like the peace the world gives. So don't be troubled or afraid" (John 14:27).

*Fifth, God will help you be able to comfort others.* Your experience of suffering will deepen your compassion for and ability to help others who suffer. Paul wrote to the Corinthians, "[God] comforts us in all our troubles so that we can comfort others. When others are troubled, we will be able to give them the same comfort God has given us. You can be sure that the more we suffer for Christ, the more God will shower us with his comfort through Christ" (2 Corinthians 1:4-5). You will be able to be a great comfort to others because you have been comforted by God through your trial.

I have seen this time and time again. You see, God is preparing you, just like those logs, for a "choice work." So what is the cause of all of our problems? Sin. What is the solution? Trust in God. Becoming a believer will not take away all the problems in your life—but it gives you new perspective, new trust, and new hope in what God is going to do in and through you as a result of every difficulty you encounter.

## SEEKING GUIDANCE

Does God still speak to people today? Is he interested in what happens to you? Does he indeed have a master plan for your life? If so, how do you discover it? How do you know the will of God? How do you hear his voice? How do you find the guidance you need for your future as a believer?

These are important questions. We all need guidance in life concerning the great questions and decisions—Whom should I marry? Should I make this job change? Should I move to this new location? How does God want me to serve him with my life?

Let me say at the outset that God is indeed interested in you as an individual. He does have a master plan for your life. That plan can and should be discovered because God wants to reveal his will to you. He does still speak to people today, and he wants to speak to you.

We as Christians are not victims of chance, hoping our luck will be good or not run out. As God led men and women in Scripture, he wants to lead you.

I wish I could give you an easy "1-2-3" method on

how to know the will of God in every situation. However, in my walk with Jesus Christ for some thirty years, I have found that the will of God happened more as I took steps of faith trying to the best of my ability to live by putting the principles of Scripture into practice. There have been those times when God has clearly spoken to me in a tangible way, but most of the time I have walked through life in this journey of faith. As we will see, God's will is not an itinerary, but an attitude.

Yet clearly God does indeed guide, he does speak. We will briefly examine some of the principles of guidance. God does not play hide-and-seek. He wants to lead you even more than you want to be led. God is more concerned about keeping you in his will than you are to be kept in it.

Far too often we can make knowing God's will far too mystical and "other worldly." When I hear these preachers on television saying, "God told me, . . ." I think that a lot of what they think they heard is coming from their own fertile imaginations—or worse!

In fact, that's not a new problem. The prophet Ezekiel spoke about those who falsely represented God. "And your prophets announce false visions and speak false messages. They say, 'My message is from the Sovereign LORD,' when the LORD hasn't spoken a single word to them. They repair cracked walls with whitewash!" (Ezekiel 22:28).

As a new believer, you can trust that God indeed

will speak to you, and you can know that the voice is his. I have found that there are concrete, practical steps that I can take to cause God's will to be more easily known to me.

## Walking in God's Will

God's way becomes plain when we start walking in it. Just as God said of Abraham, "Should I hide my plan from Abraham?" (Genesis 18:17), so God *wants* to reveal his plans to you. Abraham was called God's friend, and you are also called God's friend. Jesus said to his followers, "I no longer call you servants, because a master doesn't confide in his servants. Now you are my friends, since I have told you everything the Father told me" (John 15:15). Friends share secrets with friends. They confide in one another. So you can confide in God, and he will reveal his will to you—a will that may seem secret, but really isn't. It is important to understand your close relationship with God because there are many voices calling you to go this way or that way. Your friends, your coworkers, your boss, your family members will all have their share of advice. So how do you hear the voice of God over the din?

The Bible promises that, as followers of Jesus, we are like sheep following our shepherd. Listen to what Jesus said, "A shepherd enters through the gate. . . . The sheep hear his voice and come to him. . . . They follow him because they recognize his voice" (John

10:2-4). You can rest on that promise that, as Jesus' follower, you *will* recognize his voice.

The Bible gives many passages that clearly show the will of God for every individual. God wants you to follow the directions he has already given in Scripture.

Some believers may complain that God seems silent and they can't get an answer from him. It could be that God is waiting to reveal his specific plans for them because he is waiting for them to act on what he has already revealed in Scripture! Sometimes believers are crying out for God to show them his will when they are holding his will right in their hands—in God's Word.

Let's say you were having trouble programming your VCR (doesn't everybody?). So you decide that you need the people at the electronics store to somehow transmit a special message to your mind so you can know how to get "12:00" from blinking constantly.

That is ridiculous.

What you need to do is open up that pesky little book called the "User's Manual" and follow the instructions. In the same way, as a Christian who wants to know God's will for your life, you need to look at what God has already written in life's User's Manual—the Bible. Your obedience to what God has already revealed in his Word guarantees that he will give guidance in matters that are not so clear.

Let's consider a few foundational principles:

*First, in order to know God's will, you must be a believer.* The first point will seem obvious, but if you miss it, all the other points will be of no real value. God does not clearly show his will to those who are not in a personal relationship with him. Remember the shepherd and the sheep? Only those who are part of Jesus' flock will hear and know his voice. The Bible reminds us that God is "not willing that any should perish but that all should come to repentance" (2 Peter 3:9, NKJV).

*Second, in order to know God's will, you need to be filled with the Holy Spirit.* Ephesians 5:17 says, "Therefore do not be foolish, but understand what the Lord's will is" (NIV). How do you understand that will of the Lord? Read on: Ephesians 5:18 says, "Don't be drunk with wine, because that will ruin your life. Instead, let the Holy Spirit fill and control you" (Ephesians 5:18). Or as the King James Version puts it, "Be filled with the Spirit." It is significant that Paul writes that believers should "be filled with the Spirit." In the Greek, this phrase is in the present tense, as in "constantly be filled." This is also a command. It is the will of God that every believer constantly be filled with the Holy Spirit.

*Third, God's will is that his people live pure lives.* Paul wrote to the Thessalonians regarding knowing God's will: "It is *God's will* that you should be sanctified: that you should avoid sexual immorality"

(1 Thessalonians 4:3, NIV, emphasis mine). To be "sanctified" means to be made holy, to be dedicated to God. This speaks to single people to remain sexually pure until marriage, and to married people to be faithful to their spouse. There are no exceptions to this rule of Scripture. In other words, if you are seeking God's guidance about whether to have sex before marriage, or whether to leave your spouse for someone else—then look at Scripture and you don't have to look far. The answer, clear as day, is *no.* God will never lead you in a way contrary to what he has already said in his Word. Period.

*Fourth, God's will is that his people have an attitude of gratitude.* "No matter what happens, always be thankful, for *this is God's will* for you who belong to Christ Jesus" (1 Thessalonians 5:18, emphasis mine). This simply refers to an attitude that recognizes that God is in control of all circumstances that surround your life. It understands that God leads to still waters as well as stormy seas. Everything that happens in your life is part of the process of making you more like Jesus.

## Following God's Plan

Having established what his will is for all his followers in some areas of life and seeking to follow that, you can then proceed to seeking God's specific direction for your life. James writes, "If you need wisdom—if you want to know what God wants you to do—ask him, and he will gladly tell you. He will not resent your asking. But when you ask him, be sure that you really expect him to answer, for a doubtful mind is as unsettled as a wave of the sea that is driven and tossed by the wind" (James 1:5-6). So ask God for wisdom— for today's activities, for tomorrow's situations, for next year's goals. He may not give you every detail, but you can trust that he will give you enough guidance to bring you along the right path to his planned destination. A Jewish proverb says, "It is better to ask the way ten times than to take the wrong road once."

Now let's look at some steps you can take to "prepare the ground" to hear the voice of God and know his will. We're going to look at Romans 12:1-2.

> I beseech you therefore, brethren, by the mercies of God, that you present your bodies a living sacrifice, holy, acceptable to God, which is your reasonable service. And do not be conformed to this world, but be transformed by the renewing of your mind, that you may prove what is that good and acceptable and perfect will of God. (NKJV)

Notice the order in these verses. You must first be "a living sacrifice," then you will discover "that good and acceptable and perfect will of God." We tend to want to know his will first, and then we will decide if we will give ourselves to it. But in essence, God says, "Give me your life, and I will show you my will." It is when we learn this lesson that we are ready for an exciting life of God continually unfolding his will for us.

To present your body as a "living sacrifice" refers to an offering, something you do willingly. God wants the heartfelt gift of your life, time, and resources—not out of duty, but out of love. You can hang around as a believer who doesn't want to give everything totally to God. You can hold back, but in so doing, you miss out on all the benefits of complete surrender to Jesus Christ, including discovering his perfect will for your life. If you want to do all that God has in mind for you to do, then you need to surrender completely to him. You'll never be totally happy, fulfilled, and content until you do!

To "not be conformed to this world" means not loving that world system that is spiritually bankrupt and hostile to God. The Greek word for "conform" refers to the act of assuming an outward appearance that does not accurately reflect what is within. In other words, Paul was saying, "Don't masquerade as if you belong to the world. That would be patterning yourself inconsistently with who you really are." John wrote, "Stop loving this evil world and all that it offers you, for when you love the world, you show that you do not have the love of the Father in you" (1 John 2:15). In a day when it is acceptable to openly mock and deride Christians, it can be a real temptation *not* to stand up for what you believe. Near the end of his life Paul wrote to Timothy, "If we endure hardship, we will reign with him. If we deny him, he will deny us" (2 Timothy 2:12). It may be difficult, but the rewards for standing up for Christ are well worth it! Jesus himself said, "If a person is ashamed of me and my message in these adulterous and sinful days, I, the Son of Man, will be ashamed of that person when I return in the glory of my Father with the holy angels" (Mark 8:38).

As you desire to know God's will, much of this world's thinking will try to cloud your reason. For instance, if you are having problems in your marriage or you become attracted to someone other than your mate, you could say, as much of the world does, "I'll get a divorce." Our culture has made divorce easy and acceptable. But as a believer, however, you need to be transformed from the world's warped and selfish way of thinking. Your mind will be transformed as you let the Holy Spirit work in your life, as you study God's Word, and as you fellowship with God's people. When your mind has been transformed by God, he will then show you his will for you. Scripture clearly teaches God wants our marriages to flourish and grow. So you choose to follow what Scripture teaches and in doing so you reject conformity to this world and its self-indulgent ways. When you do this, you are being transformed into the image of Jesus and you will find God's purpose for you!

Someone once asked a concert violinist in New York's Carnegie Hall how she became so skilled. She said that her skill was because of "planned neglect." In other words, she had planned to neglect everything that was not related to her goal. As believers, our goal is to become like Christ. With the help and guidance of the Holy Spirit, we too should set aside everything that would hinder us from reaching that goal. That's what Paul did. He wrote, "I press on toward the goal to win the prize for which God has called me heavenward in Christ Jesus" (Philippians 3:14, NIV).

To find "that good and acceptable and perfect will of God," it helps to first realize that God's will for us is good! Some people have a warped concept of God as being some kind of "celestial party-pooper" who is just waiting for them to surrender their wills to him so he can make them miserable! Nothing could be farther from the truth. The psalmist wrote, "Taste and see that the LORD is good. Oh, the joys of those who trust in him!" (Psalm 34:8).

## Listening for God's Voice

### God Speaks through His Word

As we noted in chapter 3, the basics that you need to know and the will of God for every believer are found in the Bible. In addition, even for specific situations, you can follow the general principles of God's Word, always knowing that he will never guide you in a manner that is contrary to his written Word. The Bible is your litmus test, your bedrock, your absolute. The Bible is the clear revelation by which to measure all other so-called "revelations." It is the rock of stability on which to test your fickle emotions. The way you will know what is right or wrong is by looking to see what Scripture says. Everything you need to know is found in its pages. "All Scripture is inspired by God and is useful to teach us what is true and to make us realize what is wrong in our lives. It straightens us out and teaches us to do what is right" (2 Timothy 3:16).

This does not mean that you hold your Bible up to the wind and say, "Speak to me, Lord." You need to read and study the Bible, understanding what it says in the context. There is always the danger of misinterpreting the Word or taking it out of its proper context. That's why you need to continue to study, read, and learn. Some people try to take one verse and build an entire case around it. The problem is, if their case contradicts other parts of Scripture, then their case is wrong.

### God Speaks through Circumstances

God told a young man named Gideon that he was to lead the people into battle. Gideon asked the Lord to confirm it. He put a fleece on the ground and asked the Lord to allow the fleece to be damp and the ground dry in the morning. It happened just as he asked. Then Gideon reversed it, asking that the fleece be dry and the ground be damp, and God confirmed it again (Judges 6:37-40). While this is not the best way to determine God's will, it does make a point. If the Lord is in it, he will confirm it.

Another example, God told Philip to go into the desert. God didn't give him a detailed itinerary, just a command to go, and Philip went. God's will for Philip was confirmed by what occurred when Philip obeyed (Acts 8:26-39). God's will for Jonah was certainly revealed through the whale! Jonah thought he'd make different travel plans, but God's will was for Jonah to go to Nineveh (Jonah 1:1-17)! Paul was guided, stopped, and moved by dreams, shipwrecks, even sickness. Even people can be a part of God's plan to guide you.

### God Speaks in Your Heart

You might call this a "spiritual stirring." You sense that something is happening. You have a great peace that could come only from God. "And let the peace that comes from Christ rule in your hearts. For as members of one body you are all called to live in peace. And always be thankful" (Colossians 3:15). This could be more literally translated, "Let the peace of God act as an umpire in your hearts, settling with finality all matters that arise."

F. B. Meyer has given some practical advice on discerning God's leading. He writes, "When I was crossing the Irish Channel one starless night, I stood on the deck by the captain and asked him, 'How do you know Holyhead Harbor on so dark a night as this?' He said, 'You see those three lights? All of them must line up together as one, and when we see them so unite, we know the exact position of the harbor's mouth.'"

Meyer concludes that when we want to know God's will, three things must always line up, like those lights in the harbor. The three things are:

1. The inward impulse
2. The Word of God
3. The trend of circumstances

God is in the heart, compelling you forward; God is in his book, corroborating whatever he says in your heart; and God is in circumstances, indicating his will. Never start until these three things agree.

I would add that there is also the issue of God's timing. The Bible says, "He has made everything beautiful in its time" (Ecclesiastes 3:11, NIV). In short:

- If the request is wrong, God will say, "No."
- If the timing is wrong, God will say, "Slow."
- If you are wrong, God will say, "Grow."
- But if the request is right, the timing is right, and you are right, God says, "Go!"

God *wants* to enter into friendship with you. He *wants* to reveal his plans to you. He *wants* to make himself known to you. He has a unique, custom-made plan for your life. You are not a mere statistic or blip on the screen. You are not the result of an evolutionary process. You are a person made in the very image of God himself.

God's will is not only good, it is also perfect. No plan of yours can improve on the plan of God. You see only bits and pieces; he sees the whole. You see only fragments of the past. You measure things by the narrow horizon of your present vision. God sees the past, present, and future in their total context as related to eternity. So don't be afraid to completely surrender to the will of God for your life. Don't be afraid to say, along with Jesus, "I want your will, not mine" (Luke 22:42). Don't be afraid to commit an unknown future to a known God. You may not know what the future holds, but you know who holds the future, and that's really all you need to know!

## SHARING MY FAITH

As followers of Jesus Christ, we have all been called to take the life-changing message of the gospel and share it with others. Jesus told his followers, "Go and make disciples of all the nations." (Matthew 28:19). By the way, his command is known as the Great Commission not the Great Suggestion! But the way many believers respond to Christ's command would make you think it was the latter instead of the former. In others words, sharing this message with others is not an option, nor is it a unique calling limited to a few special people. Every believer is called upon by Jesus himself to take this message to a lost and dying world.

"Hold on right there," you may be saying. "I'm just brand-new at this whole Christian thing. I don't know how to share my faith with anybody!"

Well, I beg to differ with you. You don't need to have an advanced theological degree to share your faith. You don't need to be a great speaker or a winning debater.

Let me ask you something. Let's say you had been diagnosed with an incurable, fatal illness. But then you found a doctor who was able to cure you! Would you not give that doctor's name to anyone and everyone who had the same disease?

Well, you *did* have a disease—it's called "sin." And that disease is always 100 percent fatal. "The wages of sin is death" (Romans 6:23). But then you found the cure! "If we confess our sins to him, he is faithful and just to forgive us and to cleanse us from every wrong" (1 John 1:9). You accepted Jesus as your Savior and now you won't face eternal death—you have been given eternal life. "The free gift of God is eternal life through Christ Jesus our Lord" (Romans 6:23).

Don't you think you ought to pass along this information? Don't you think others would like to know?

Sure, it's scary. You don't know how people will respond; you don't want people to think you're weird; you don't want to turn people off. Well, there are lots of excuses for not sharing your faith, but none of them hold up. Why?

Well, first of all, you must remember that you are not responsible for how a person responds. Your job is merely to share. It is the Holy Spirit who ultimately works in people's hearts. You can't "make" someone a Christian. You share your faith and God does the rest.

What do you share? The Bible tells us simply: "If you are asked about your Christian hope, always be ready to explain it. But you must do this in a gentle and respectful way" (1 Peter 3:15-16).

Think about it. What is *your* story? What did God do for *you?* Only you can tell that story.

## A Changed Heart

No, you don't need a degree in theology or public speaking in order to share your faith. All you really need is a changed heart—a heart that has been set free by Christ and now feels burdened for those around who still need to find that cure for sin. In reality, once you invite Jesus Christ into your life as Savior and Lord, you can immediately begin to tell others about your newfound faith.

The story is told in John's Gospel about a man who had been healed by Jesus. After his healing, certain religious rulers known as Pharisees challenged the man, asking him some rather complex questions about Jesus. The man's response is classic. He said, "Whether he is a sinner or not, I don't know. One thing I do know. I was blind but now I see!" (John 9:25, NIV).

That man was sharing his "personal testimony." A personal testimony is *your* story of how you came to know Jesus Christ. Every believer, including yourself, has a personal testimony. Now granted, your story may not be as dramatic as some others, but it is still that personal record of how you, who had once been blind, came to see.

The purpose of the testimony is essentially to give the gospel without getting into a person's face. It's a way to build a bridge, not burn one. Your objective is to try to put yourself in the shoes of the person to whom you're speaking. You are telling your own story of how you came to faith, and in doing so, you are sharing the feelings and first impressions and questions you had—which may be the very ones the person you are speaking to is having.

It is important to remember that when you share your testimony, you should never glorify or exaggerate the past. Put it in its proper context (remember, "I was blind, but now I see"). Don't focus on "What I've done for God," but rather on "What God has done for me." Don't talk about "What I gave up for God"; rather, tell others "What God gave up for me."

Another pitfall to avoid is lapsing into what I call "Christianese." That means speaking in Christianity's terminology, which makes no sense to nonbelievers. For instance, a believer, in attempting to share his testimony, might say, "I have been redeemed, washed in the blood, and sanctified by Jesus! I used to be 'in the flesh,' but now I'm a part of the body of Christ!"

"Hmm, let me understand this," the nonbeliever demurs. "You used to be 'in the flesh' but now you're in the body? And now you have been 'washed in blood'?"

See what I mean by avoiding "Christianese"?

Don't get me wrong, I am not suggesting that you not use biblical terminology when it comes to sharing your faith. I am suggesting that you try to take the biblical concepts and put them into everyday language that people can understand. For instance, Jesus often spoke in parables, which essentially were heavenly stories with earthly meaning. They were illustrations. For instance, Jesus would compare the kingdom of God to a farmer going out to plant some seed (Matthew 13:3), a sight that would be familiar to the people of his day. Such a comparison helped his listeners to understand what he was saying. You can follow his example

You also need to be tactful when you share. *Tact* is the intuitive knowledge of saying the right thing at the right time. Unfortunately, many believers have about as much tact as a bull in a china shop! I read about a barber who, as a young Christian, attended a church meeting where the speaker stressed the need to share the gospel with others. The young barber knew he was lacking in this area, so he determined that he would speak to the first person who came into his barber shop.

The next morning, after his first customer had been seated and the apron tucked around his neck, the barber began to strap his razor vigorously. Then as he tested the sharpness of the edge, he turned to the man in the chair and asked, "Friend, are you ready to die and meet God?"

The man looked at the razor and fled out the door—apron and all!

It's worth noting that even the great apostle Paul

himself constantly used his personal testimony when it came to sharing the gospel. He would start with his own story of coming to faith in Christ, and then he beat a quick path to the gospel message itself. Consider that the apostle Paul was a brilliant orator and communicator. He was deeply schooled in biblical law as well as the wisdom of Greece. If anyone could have leaned on his intellect, it would have been Paul. But he often simply told his personal story.

Sharing your personal story is a great way to get a conversation started. You may not know all the answers to someone's questions. You may not be able to answer the tough challenges that some people will throw at you. But you can say this, "I know that I was blind, and now I can see!"

There are a few things that you need to realize about every person. Everyone out there is essentially lonely, empty, guilty, and afraid to die. Now people may hide behind a convincing facade, but the truth is, they have these concerns. It doesn't matter if the person is "down and out" or "up and out." It doesn't matter if the person has hit bottom or is "king of the world." Every person is facing these concerns.

You may see someone who appears to have it all together and think he or she would never want to hear the gospel. But that is not necessarily true.

I remember, before I was a Christian, that I did a convincing job of making Christians think I would never listen to their message. The fact was, however, that I was secretly hoping one of them would talk to me. There are plenty of people out there right now who are the same way. The people around you may not appear to need anything, so it's easy to pass them by without sharing the gospel. But don't forget that once you were one of those people, and someone took the time to share with you.

People are spiritually empty. Look around, read a newspaper or magazine, and you'll discover people constantly searching—for peace, security, some kind of spirituality. They're trying everything, looking to the eastern mystics, the occult, or somewhere deep within themselves. They're not going to truly fill that emptiness until they find Christ. You can make the introduction!

People are also very lonely. Oh, they may look content, happy, wealthy, famous, and well-loved, but so many such people would attest to a deep loneliness. The great physicist Albert Einstein once wrote to a friend, "It is strange to be known so universally and yet be so lonely." Clearly, fame is no cure for that deep inner loneliness. You can tell them about a forever Friend!

People are also guilty. Every person you meet has the fatal disease of sin that only Christ can cure. The Bible tells us that "all have sinned; all fall short of God's glorious standard" (Romans 3:23). Every person sins; every person experiences guilt. Some feel more shame than others. Some are good at rationalizing; others attempt to hide behind alcohol or other substances or addictions. They may not think about it much, but they know, deep down, that they are out of sync with the Creator. You know the cure for the guilt!

Most people are afraid to die. We don't even like to use the word. If someone dies, we don't use "the D word." We say that the person has "passed away" or "passed on" or "is no longer with us." People are afraid of death. The Bible speaks of those who are "held in slavery by their fear of death" (Hebrews 2:15, NIV). The only way to have true peace about death is to know what lies beyond it. God has told us what is beyond the grave for those who love him. You can share with people your new assurance about God's future plans for you. Jesus said, "I am the resurrection and the life. Those who believe in me, even though they die like everyone else, will live again" (John 11:25).

Your new faith, your new assurances, and your changed life and heart will attest to the power of the Holy Spirit within you. And that power, working through you, can have a life-changing effect on others.

## God's Leading

An exciting aspect of the Christian life is the knowledge that you are now God's instrument to make a difference in the world! He may use you to lead hundreds of thousands to Christ; he may use you to lead a couple of your friends, your children, your family members. You don't need to run around worrying about trying to find people; instead, you need to be open to God's leading. He will guide you to people who need to hear what you have to say. He will be working in their hearts, making them ready to hear you.

An example of being available for God to use in found in the Bible in Acts 8. Philip had been chosen to be in charge of food distribution in the early church (Acts 6:5). Clearly, he was open to letting God use him wherever God chose. After his coworker Stephen was martyred, Philip went to Samaria and had quite a ministry (Acts 8:5-8). But then one day God inexplicably called him to go down to some desert road between Jerusalem and Gaza. That doesn't exactly sound like a place for a huge ministry. But Philip obeyed.

God will indeed call you. You may experience a tug on your heart; you may find yourself in a situation with a person asking a question; you may just feel that you are supposed to be in a certain place. This "impression" or "burden" may come in the form of an impelling desire to talk to someone about your faith. Follow those urgings. God may have a special appointment for you to keep.

However, you don't need to wait to be sure you've heard from God before you share your faith. God has already commanded you to go and preach the gospel. You should take advantage of every opportunity.

In the case of Philip, the Bible says, "An angel of

the Lord spoke to Philip, saying, 'Arise and go toward the south along the road which goes down from Jerusalem to Gaza.' This is desert" (Acts 8:26, NKJV).

One might not be surprised if Philip would have argued with the angel. "What? Leave this revival we're having in Samaria to go to the desert? For what? I'm eighty miles from where you want me to go. The apostles and other believers are at least thirty miles closer, so why don't you just use one of them? I'm not the only Christian around!"

There were two roads from Jerusalem to Gaza. The angel commanded Philip to take the one that was seldom used. It is possible to translate the Greek phrase "toward the south" as "at noon." In other words, God was saying, "Not only do I want you to go out to the desert to a basically unused road, I want you to go in the hottest time of the day."

There are times when the Lord may lead you in a way that does not seem logical at the moment. But Philip trusted that God knew exactly what he was doing. We also see from the story that God had uniquely prepared both the subject Philip would be speaking about as well as Philip himself!

God has uniquely prepared you as well! And when God says, "Go," he sees the big picture while you are limited to the small one. God doesn't usually give a detailed blueprint, but instead will lead you one step at a time. If you are unwilling to take the first step, don't expect him to give you the second!

So Philip went down to that dusty road (it was a long, hot walk) and came across a man in a chariot. That man happened to be "the treasurer of Ethiopia, a eunuch of great authority under the queen of Ethiopia. The eunuch had gone to Jerusalem to worship, and he was now returning" (Acts 8:27-28). Philip had never met this man, and surely had no idea of the openness of his heart. But God knew, and God made an appointment that resulted in the conversion of that man who "went on his way rejoicing" (Acts 8:39).

## A Simple Message

The heartbeat of the gospel message is the story of the life, death, and resurrection of Jesus Christ. Don't ever forget the simplicity of the gospel. As already mentioned, there is a place for the personal testimony. But the heartbeat, the bottom line of what you are saying is the simple yet profound gospel message.

This word "gospel" means good news. But before people can fully appreciate the good news, they need to first know the bad news.

The bad news is that we are all sinners and that our sin separates us from God. Jesus came to bring God and people together. When he died on the cross, the sins of the whole world were placed upon him, and the penalty for those sins was paid in full. Three days after his crucifixion, he rose from the dead, proving that he was the true Son of God, the only one who could pay for our sins.

Although the message is simple, it is incredibly powerful. Paul wrote, "I am not ashamed of this Good News about Christ. It is the power of God at work, saving everyone who believes" (Romans 1:16).

The word for "power" is a Greek word that means "explosive dynamic power." In other words, there is this built-in power in the simple yet life-changing message of the gospel. Don't underestimate it, or feel that you need to add to or take away from it. Instead, you need to deliver the gospel with clarity and compassion.

You will do well to remember that Christians are just like one beggar telling another beggar where to find bread. Christians are not better than nonbelievers (although we are clearly "better-off"!). Someone once asked the great British preacher C. H. Spurgeon, if he could put in a few words what his Christian faith was all about. Spurgeon said, "I will put it into four words for you: Christ died for me."

Here are the basics of the gospel message that you can share with people. I want to introduce two significant words that you need to know: justification and adoption.

### Justification

"Justification" is used often in the New Testament to describe what salvation brings. Romans 8:30 says, "And those he predestined, he also called; those he called, he also justified; those he justified, he also glorified" (NIV). Romans 5:1-2 says, "Therefore, since we have been justified through faith, we have peace with God through our Lord Jesus Christ, through whom we have gained access by faith into this grace in which we now stand. And we rejoice in the hope of the glory of God" (NIV).

If people really understand the meaning of "justification," it can quite literally change their lives. The word "justify" carries a two-fold meaning. First, it speaks of the forgiveness of sins. The day people put their faith in Jesus Christ is the day their sins will be instantly forgiven! Don't rush over that idea; let your listeners think about it. Let it sink in.

You can ask, "Have you done things you are ashamed of? Things you wish you had never done?" Then explain that because of Jesus' death on the cross, they are 100 percent forgiven! Speaking of sins, God says, "[Your] sins and lawless acts I will remember no more" (Hebrews 10:17, NIV). The Old Testament prophet Jeremiah wrote, "I . . . will never again remember their sins" (Jeremiah 31:34). According to God's Word, when people believe in Jesus, their sins are *gone!* God has released them from the guilt and penalty of the sins they have committed. God has taken their sins, thrown them into the "Sea of Forgetfulness," and posted a sign that reads, "No fishing allowed!"

It is important to let people know that God does not wish them to remember what he is willing to forget. God has a big eraser, and he uses it to remove all the sins of those who put their trust in Jesus Christ.

157

If that is all salvation was, it would be more than we could ever hope for. But that is only one part of justification. For justification does not only speak of what God has taken away, it also speaks of what he has put in its place. Justification is more than just forgiveness and the removal of the guilt and condemnation that accompanied it. Justification has a positive side as well, which includes what Christ has done and given to people. The word "justified" means "to put to one's account." When God justifies people, he does so by placing to their credit all the righteousness of Christ. In essence, he balances their moral and spiritual budget—deducting their sin and crediting Christ's righteousness.

This is not a gradual process. It is immediate. Instantaneous. It would be as though a person were in debt for ten million dollars, the creditors were at the door, and there was no hope to ever repay this enormous debt. Then, unexpectedly, a very wealthy person came along and paid the debt. A person would be happy enough to simply no longer be in debt, but this benefactor also added twenty million dollars to the person's account!

In the same way, God has justified people. It has nothing to do with their worthiness or performance. It has everything to do with Jesus, who has paid the price for their sins. When they accept him, he takes up residence in their hearts. Their new value and position are all because of what Jesus has done for them!

Justification is not about what they have done for God. It's about what God has done for them.

What is the result of this wonderful work? They are at peace with God, having free access into his presence and the hope of glory!

But wait there's more!

### Adoption

Tell them that they are also *adopted* into God's family. Justification has to do with a change in standing. Adoption has to do with a change in position. Adoption means "the placing of a child." It is more than enough to know that God has forgiven them of all their sins and that he has made them right before him. But then, he takes them into his family as his own children!

Ephesians 1:5 says, "His unchanging plan has always been to adopt us into his own family by bringing us to himself through Jesus Christ. And this gave him great pleasure." Galatians 4:4-5 says, "But when the right time came, God sent his Son, born of a woman, subject to the law. God sent him to buy freedom for us who were slaves to the law, so that he could adopt us as his very own children."

There they were, slaves of sin under the control of Satan. Jesus came along and bought their freedom. That's more than they could ever hope for. But then he marched them down to the courthouse and adopted them! In essence, they have been given the full rights of sonship in the family of God.

I can stand in awe of a God that has the power and desire to forgive me and then put his righteousness to my account. But by adoption, God is saying, "Don't merely stand in awe of me, come close to me!" Galatians 4:6 says, "Now you can call God your dear Father."

God wants them to know that he cares about them and that they have total and free access to his presence anytime.

## Tell the World

That was the message you heard and to which you responded. Learn the basics of this message so you can share it with others. Underline those verses in your Bible; put tabs there; be ready to share.

Although the gospel message is very simple, it obviously helps to know your Bible. While you don't need to be a Bible scholar to begin to share your faith, you do need to study God's Word consistently. The more you know, the more you'll understand and the more you'll be able to help others understand as well.

For example, let's go back to Philip on that desert road. The Bible says that the man was "reading the book of the prophet Isaiah" (Acts 8:28, NIV). Philip was led by the Spirit to walk beside this VIP's chariot and in so doing, Philip overheard the man reading.

So did Philip say, "Hey you, heathen guy, are you washed in the blood, or on your way to hell?"

No, Philip asked the man, "Do you understand what you are reading?"

There's that tact I wrote about earlier in this chapter.

Now, we can assume that Philip *did* understand, and so he was prepared to take the passage the man was reading and explain the gospel message of Jesus Christ right from that passage! Philip used the Scripture from Isaiah as a starting point. Then he used a number of other passages to tell the Ethiopian about Jesus. Philip knew God's Word, and he knew how to start right from the man's question and then tell him the simple gospel message. You may not understand everything yet, but get started studying your Bible. God will use what you learn, I guarantee it!

As the Spirit leads you to people, take the time to find out where they are at and what they are thinking. What questions do they have? You start there, trying to establish common ground. This doesn't mean that you change or adapt the truth of the message; you simply acknowledge that although people are essentially the same—empty, lonely, guilty, and afraid to die—they are at different stages in life and facing their own unique joys and challenges. If you're going to share the gospel message with someone, you need to be willing to put yourself in that person's shoes for a moment and express yourself so that you can be understood.

For example, Jesus, the master communicator, never dealt with any two people in exactly the same way. The woman at the well had spent a lifetime trying to fill a void with men. Jesus spoke of her deep spiritual thirst (John 4). To an expert in theology, however, Jesus spoke in almost childlike terms as he told Nicodemus that he had to be born again (John 3).

Keep this point in mind whenever you are talking to someone about the gospel. Establish a relationship, and then, based on what you learn, ask yourself how you can connect this person's need with Christ. Let the Spirit guide your words and help you build a bridge between the person's need and the simple message of the gospel.

## What's Next?

You have embarked on an amazing adventure called the Christian life! God will use you to help build his kingdom. He wants to use your story to help tell his story and bring more people into his kingdom. You are a part of that work. Your story is important. But God wants more than just your story.

Hopefully, when you became a believer, someone came alongside to help you. We call that "discipling" another person. Just as a newborn baby is cared for and nurtured, so a newborn believer needs to be cared for and taught as he or she grows. Someone cared for you; you need to care for others. There will be some to whom you will tell your story and they go on their way, seemingly unchanged. Maybe you'll never see them again. We say that you have "planted a seed" that perhaps someone else will be able to water and make grow.

There will be others, however, whom you will have the awesome privilege of joining as they walk into Christ's kingdom. You need to be ready to take on a commitment to help that person grow in Christ. Of course, you'll be growing together, but you can share what you learn with him or her. In fact, no believer is totally mature until he or she gets to heaven. We're all works in process; we're all learning from God and from one another.

To disciple someone means to live out your faith, to teach it by your word, and to model it by your example. To the best of your ability, you help other new believers get up on their feet and become spiritually mature. You will need to take great care to nurture, protect, and guide anyone whom you lead to Christ.

Right after I made my personal commitment to Christ, I was very vulnerable spiritually. Unfortunately, nobody really told me the significance of what I had done or what it really meant to follow Christ. I was uncomfortable around my old nonbelieving friends, but I was still a little mystified by the Christians whom I did not fully understand. Then the Lord led a person named Mark to me. He came up to me after school one day and said, "Didn't you make a commitment to Christ a few days ago?"

I looked around suspiciously and murmured, "Yes."

Mark told me I needed a Bible and should go to church. But he took the next step and gave me that Bible and personally took me to church with him. He became a friend who helped me in those first awkward months of new belief. He modeled for me what a Christian was like in the real world. He introduced me to other believers and was one of the first ones to teach me the basics of the Bible.

In short, Mark discipled me, and I thank God for it. You need to do the same for others. You may never reach thousands or hundreds, but you may reach one. And who knows what God will do with that one person to change our world!

So come on. Let's go fishing for people!

You (and they) will never be the same for it. And that is a good thing!